SOUND ADVICE

SOUND ADVICE
A Basis for Listening

Stacy A. Hagen

Edmonds Community College
and the University of Washington

with illustrations by Eric Deeter

PRENTICE HALL REGENTS, Englewood Cliffs, New Jersey 07632

Library of Congress Cataloging-in-Publication Data

HAGEN, STACY A.
   Sound advice: a basis for listening/Stacy A. Hagen; with
illustrations by Eric Deeter.
      p. cm.
   ISBN 0-13-823154-0: $8.00
   1. English language—Textbooks for foreign speakers.
2. Listening. 3. English language—Spoken English. I. Title.
PE1128.H227 1988   87-32626
428.3'4—dc19   CIP

Editorial/production supervision and
   interior design: Arthur Maisel
Cover design: Wanda Lubelska Design
Manufacturing buyer: Margaret Rizzi

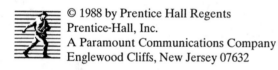 © 1988 by Prentice Hall Regents
Prentice-Hall, Inc.
A Paramount Communications Company
Englewood Cliffs, New Jersey 07632

Printed in the United States of America

10

ISBN   0-13-823154-0

Prentice-Hall International (UK) Limited, *London*
Prentice-Hall of Australia Pty. Limited, *Sydney*
Prentice-Hall Canada Inc., *Toronto*
Prentice-Hall Hispanoamericana, S.A., *Mexico*
Prentice-Hall of India Private Limited, *New Delhi*
Prentice-Hall of Japan, Inc., *Tokyo*
Simon & Schuster Asia Pte. Ltd., *Singapore*
Editora Prentice-Hall do Brasil, Ltda., *Rio de Janeiro*

for M.D.R.
whose wisdom, talent, and love made this work possible

Contents

Preface

Sound Advice: A Basis for Listening presents a skills approach to discrete-point listening. Designed for intermediate and advanced students, it covers a variety of listening phenomena essential for the comprehension of authentic, natural speech—what ESL students generally refer to as "fast English."

Through systematic practice with such phenomena as linking, assimilation, and reduced speech, students gain accuracy in understanding frequent, yet troublesome aspects of listening comprehension. Easier, more general concepts are introduced first and spiraled throughout, as students progress to more demanding ones. Explanations, accompanied by easy-to-read sound representations, are presented in a clear, concise format. Carefully controlled and sequenced exercises expose students to a variety of colloquial, natural sounding English. Beginning at the word and sentence level, and expanding to short exchanges and conversations, students develop strategies rather than memorize set phrases, to understand the language as it is spoken.

Students preparing for the TOEFL test will find this material thorough preparation for Parts A and B of the listening section. Sentence paraphrase and/or TOEFL-style exchanges can be found at the end of Chapters 2–11; Chapters 12, 13, and 14 simulate Parts A and B of the listening portion of the test.

Whether the source be TV, radio, or a casual encounter, students are regularly frustrated by rapid, relaxed speech. Even university-bound students trained in academic listening are often at a loss when trying to respond to authentic, extended discourse. Detailed listening training can markedly enhance students' recognition of natural speech phenomena, an important part of their overall communicative competence.

Acknowledgments

No text is solely the work of its author. I would therefore like to acknowledge those who contributed so generously to this book.

A sincere thanks to my students, whose spirit, support, and candid feedback guided this process throughout; and to the administration of the Intensive ESL Program, for its recognition of and respect for ESL instruction.

My appreciation to Suzanne Cloke, Joyce Kruithof, and Daphne Mackey for field testing the material and providing valued input.

My gratitude to Eric Deeter, whose artistic excellence made the project far more enjoyable than I ever imagined.

Many thanks to Steven Weinberger who so willingly lent his expertise on very short notice.

A special thanks to Michael Legutke, for his careful reading of the manuscript, thoughtful suggestions, and encouragement.

My appreciation to Barbara Griffeth for her attentive and detailed proofreading.

My gratitude to Pat Grogan, for first encouraging me to submit the material, and then for her patient and wise counsel.

A lasting thanks to my mother, Patricia Hagen, and my father, Robert Hagen, for teaching me the value of the written word.

My appreciation to Brenda White and Arthur Maisel, ESL Editor and Production Editor respectively, whose advice, availability, and attention to detail made a painful process as painless as possible.

Lastly, I am indebted to Nancy Casey and Scott Newcombe, for their unfailing friendship, encouragement, and insight, both professional and otherwise—no matter what the hour or need.

To the Teacher

Overview

Sound Advice: A Basis for Listening is designed for intermediate/high intermediate to advanced students. Although the material can be covered successfully in one term, teachers may wish to allow two terms if the material is used largely as a supplement. Many of the exercises are appropriate for self-study in the language lab, so lab use is encouraged. This will allow a class to progress more quickly through the material. (See Instructor's Manual for exercises appropriate for lab use.) Chapters 12, 13, and 14 are geared toward students preparing for the TOEFL Test and can be done solely in the language lab if time presents a problem.

The focus is on discrete-point rather than global skills. Subject matter is arranged beginning with the easier, more general concepts and moving to those which are more specific and demanding. Since authentic, extended discourse presents a formidable challenge to nonnative speakers, the points are introduced in manageable chunks. The material spirals so that phenomena found in previous chapters will be reviewed in subsequent ones. It is recommended that the chapters be covered in order.

The exercises do not encourage immediate pronunciation of chapter material. Since receptive skills precede productive ones, it is essential that students gain receptive familiarity before they incorporate the patterns into their own speech. Once this occurs, much of the material can be used for pronunciation practice.

Instructors may wish to treat Chapter 8, "Listening for Function Words," as a supplementary chapter, depending on student needs. Beginning in Chapter 1, students have worked with function words, but, because these words occur with such frequency, I feel an entire chapter devoted to their review is appropriate in the latter part of the text. My experience has been that, while many students are quite adept at distinguishing among these words after working through the other chapters, some still require a more focused review.

Exercise Presentation

The following suggestions reflect an approach I have found successful; however, diverse teaching styles allow a variety of methods, and it is by no means the sole one.

Each chapter begins with simple listening practice, where students either attend to or mark the target structures. It is important that they have exposure to the new concepts before they are asked to apply them. Students may need to hear the introductory sentences several times before they begin to feel familiar with a particular concept. For the exercises, I recommend students hear sentences at least twice.

MAKING INFERENCES.   Students hear a sentence or short exchange and read a related question:

A. What's happening?

B: We're just waiting for our order.

Q: Where might this conversation take place?

Possible answers include "a fast-food restaurant," or "a store." Responses should be given orally; some instructors, however, may wish to provide the class with a minute or two to write down answers if there are students who are quite vocal or tend to dominate. Students can then present them orally for discussion.

CREATING CONTEXTS.   Students hear a single sentence or short exchange and suggest a possible context, generally regarding speaker, setting, time, or mood.

A: Are the eggs ready?

B: They're getting there.

A logical context is that one person is cooking and the other waiting. It could be breakfast, the speakers may be husband and wife. One of the speakers may be quite hungry or feeling impatient.

These exercises are open-ended and a variety of answers is acceptable. Again, oral discussion is preferred but students may need a few minutes to jot down answers, as mentioned above.

The "Creating Contexts" sections are designed to challenge more advanced students. If these exercises prove to be too demanding for students with weaker aural/oral skills, more structured exercise types can be found in the Instructor's Manual.

DICTATION (ORAL OR WRITTEN). Traditionally, dictations are written; this exercise, however, offers a choice between written or oral responses. If done orally, the students repeat the sentence with **slow** speech. Either style achieves the objective of having students recognize the target structures. Students are **not** being asked to replicate the structure in the form they have just heard, but rather in the longer, more careful form. One approach to student responses is to place the incorrect answers on the board and compare them with the correct response.

CONVERSATIONS. Each conversation is accompanied by an illustration, which can be used for discussion to provide a context or set the scene. The tape should be played once, before students write any responses. It can then be played again, with a pause after each phrase or sentence, to allow students to fill in the blanks.

When all answers have been completed and errors discussed, the instructor may wish to elicit conversation: e.g., "Where might the speakers be?" "How does Speaker A feel?" or "What is the relationship between speaker A and B?"

The conversations are a culmination of points previously taught and are deliberately placed at the end of a section or chapter so students have an opportunity to demonstrate their mastery of the material. Introducing them earlier may cause the teacher to resort to global skills in order to provide meaningful practice. Since *Sound Advice* teaches discrete-point rather than global listening, this would significantly alter the scope and focus of the text.

SENTENCE PARAPHRASE. This exercise is similar to Part A of the TOEFL Listening Test—the only differences being that each sentence offers three choices (the TOEFL offers four), and sentences contain specific points introduced in the chapter.

SHORT CONVERSATIONS. The majority of the blanks that students fill in contain items studied in the chapter. Often, however, phenomena found in previous chapters will be included. Again, the sentences should be played at least twice, with appropriate pauses, so that students have enough time to record their answers.

Sound-Symbol Correspondence

My primary consideration in choosing a sound-symbol representation was that it be clear and immediately accessible to students. The sound representations stay as close to the Roman alphabet as possible so that students unfamiliar with the International Phonetic Alphabet will not be at a disadvantage, and valuable time needed for listening will not be spent on mastering sound transcription.

Sound representations are indicated in italics. Boldface is used to highlight words and phrases introduced or explained in the boxes. Stressed words are indicated in capital letters.

Dialect Variation

The speech in this text is of the dialect spoken in the Central and Western regions of the U.S. It is inevitable that some sound representations in the text will differ from the instructor's speech, whether it be due to register or regional variation. As a rule of thumb, if the instructor expects students will **hear** a variation or if students themselves raise the question, alternate representations can be presented.

*   *   *

An Instructor's Manual with chapter notes and supplementary material is available free of charge to all instructors. A set of three cassette tapes can be ordered from Prentice Hall Regents, Englewood Cliffs, New Jersey 07632, USA.

SOUND ADVICE
A Basis for Listening

1 Introduction to Word and Sentence Level Reductions

Part I: Nonreleased Final Consonants

(a)	to**p**	*p*	One of the more basic problems in understanding English is non-released final consonants. When the following consonants come at the end of a word,
(b)	la**te**	*t*	
(c)	ba**ck**	*k*	$$p, t, k, b, d, g$$
(d)	ro**b**	*b*	the sound is formed but not released. **Closure** is made but the release is not heard. This may make some words in sentences hard to hear. Native speakers can tell the difference among these sounds from the closure.
(e)	ba**d**	*d*	
(f)	bi**g**	*g*	
(g)	mop/mob		If you compare (g), (h), and (i), you will see how difficult it is to tell the difference when these words are spoken in isolation.
(h)	sat/sad		
(i)	pick/pig		
(j)	He feels mad. *He feels mat.		You may have noticed that the vowel length is longer for words ending in *b*, *d*, and *g*. That can be a clue. Context will also help you, as in (j).

*Not English.

Exercise 1

Listen to the following pairs of words. Practice listening for the closure:

1. may, mate
2. tried, try
3. leap, Lee
4. fake, Fay
5. way, weight
6. play, played
7. see, seed
8. slow, slope
9. joke, Joe
10. saw, sawed
11. birthday, birth date
12. state, stay

Exercise 2

Listen to the following sentences. Notice the final sound:

1.	She acts ma**d**.	6.	He made a mistake.
2.	The tape won't sti**ck**.	7.	Maybe I should.
3.	A size ten is way too **big**.	8.	I need to take a nap.
4.	He has a broken foot.	9.	What's it about?
5.	It's store bought.	10.	Let's pay the ta**b**.

Exercise 3

Decide if the following are the same or different:

1.   same   different

2.   same   different

3.   same   different

4.   same   different

5.   same   different

6.   same   different

Exercise 4

Circle "yes" if you hear a final consonant and "no" if not:

1.   yes   no

2.   yes   no

3.   yes   no

4.   yes   no

5.   yes   no

Exercise 5 (Optional)

Same as before:

1.   yes   no

2.   yes   no

3.   yes   no

4.   yes   no

5.   yes   no

Exercise 6

Circle the word you hear. Use context to help you choose:

1.   sad   sat

2.   rip   rib

3.   bag   back

4.   bad   bat

5.   lit   lid

Exercise 7 (Optional)

Same as before:

1.   right   ride

2.   cap   cab

3.   rope   robe

4.   sag   sack

5.   at   add

Exercise 8

Fill in the blanks with the words you hear:

1.   The party was _____!

2.   We'll take a _____.

3.   Here's my _____.

4.   They just got _____.

5.   She knows it by _____.

Exercise 9 (Optional)

Same as before:

1.   Leave a _____.

2.   What a great _____!

3.   I'll write a _____.

4.   Just a little _____.

5.   What's your _____?

Part II: Syllable Stress

			Unstressed syllables are frequently reduced. This means that the sound is *uh* or *ih* (usually *uh*).*
(a)	because	buh CAUSE	
(b)	medical	MEH duh cul	Words with more than one syllable will often have reduced syllables. This makes reduced syllables very common.
(c)	polite	puh LITE	

*In dictionaries and pronunciation books, you will usually see this symbol: /ə/

Exercise 10

Listen to the following words. Mark the stressed syllable and predict the pronunciation of the reduced syllable:

1.   abóut

2.   between

3.   children

4.   color

5.   visit

6.   common

7.   believe

8.   police

9.   going

10.   hundred

11.   feeling

12.   mistake

13.   correct

14.   even

Exercise 11

Same as before:

1.	Japán	5.	marriage	9.	often
2.	escape	6.	erase	10.	woman
3.	divorce	7.	today	11.	hello
4.	behave	8.	receive	12.	resting

Exercise 12

Now you will hear three-syllable words. In three-syllable words, usually one syllable is stressed and the others are reduced. Listen to the reduced pronunciation and mark the stressed syllable:

1.	remémber	6.	tomorrow
2.	delicious	7.	returning
3.	banana	8.	hospital
4.	logical	9.	chemical
5.	animal	10.	practical

Part III: Ellipsis

(a)	terrible	terr'ble	You have learned that unstressed syllables are reduced. In words with more than two syllables, a sound is often completely dropped. This is called **ellipsis**.
(b)	chocolate	choc'late	
(c)	business	bus'ness	
(d)	probably	pro'bly	
(e)	because	'cause	Sometimes, the initial unstressed syllable can be dropped, as in (e), (f), (g), and (h).
(f)	about	'bout	
(g)	remember	'member	
(h)	exactly	'xactly	
(i)	Help yourself. There's a whole 'nother one in the oven.		An interesting form of ellipsis is "whole 'nother," meaning: "another whole." In this case, the words are reversed before ellipsis occurs. This phrase is common in **spoken** English.

Exercise 13

The following words will be spoken with reduced pronunciation. Cross out the dropped sound. (Notice that these words will not sound like the spelling.)

1. int~e~resting
2. family
3. factory
4. ordinary
5. suppose
6. finally

7. vegetables
8. separate
9. evening
10. especially
11. average
12. Florida

Exercise 14

Before you listen to the following words, try to predict how they will sound with reduced pronunciation. After you hear them, cross out the dropped syllable:

1. gen~e~rous
2. horrible
3. cabinet
4. temperature

5. different
6. aspirin
7. gasoline

8. garage
9. reference
10. favorite

Exercise 15 (Optional)

Try to predict the missing sound in each word:

Example: mathematics   *math'matics*

1. traveler   _____
2. memory   _____
3. enough   _____

4. every _____

5. another _____

6. camera _____

7. bakery _____

8. instead _____

Part IV: Function Words

		Words as well as syllables are reduced. Important words are stressed and unimportant words are reduced.
(a) **Do they** think so?	*Duh they*	Unimportant words are called **function** words. They are mainly:
(b) I disagree **with you.**	*wuth ya*	
(c) **Do you** know?	*D'ya*	articles, prepositions, pronouns, conjunctions, auxiliary verbs, "be" verbs
(d) I know **for** sure.	*fer*	
(e) Talk **to** me.	*tuh*	Important words are called **content** words. They are:
		nouns, verbs, adjectives, adverbs
		Note the reduction of the function words in (a)—(e).
(f) **News travels quickly.**		In (f), all words are content words, so there are no reductions.
(g) He was away for MONTHS. (h) He was away FOUR MONTHS.		Compare (g) and (h). The difference in meaning is determined by the stress.

Exercise 16

The following sentences will be spoken with reduced pronunciation. Before you listen, circle the words you think will be reduced:

1. Do you know that?

2. It's bigger than you think.

3. We are going there.

4. Are they new here?

5. It's more than that.

6. We wish they knew.

Exercise 17

Fill in the blanks with the words you hear. (You may want to review the information about non-released consonants in Part I.)

1. _____ leaving so soon?

2. It's all _____.

3. When _____ she be back?

4. She _____ happy _____ most part.

5. Mine _____ better _____ theirs.

Check your answers.

6. It's in _____.

7. I'll be _____.

8. What have _____?

9. We _____ there day _____ yesterday.

10. You'd better _____.

Part V: More Ellipsis: Initial Word Deletion

(a)	**Do you** care for a drink?	'care
(b)	**I beg** your pardon?	'beg
(c)	**It** sounds good.	'sounds
(d)	**Are** you leaving now?	'you
		ya
(e)	**Have you** got a minute?	'got
(f)	**Would you** mind if I open the window?	'mind

Often the first word or words in a sentence are deleted. This is another form of ellipsis.

This is common in spoken English.

Ellipsis will be studied more completely in Chapter 6.

Exercise 18

You will hear these sentences spoken with ellipsis. Repeat the complete sentences (without ellipsis) and then write the deleted words:

1. Got some extra?   *Have you*
2. Know much about it?   _____
3. Sounds expensive.   _____
4. 'Member the answer?   _____
5. Something the matter?   _____
6. Care for another one?   _____
7. Mind if I sit here?   _____
8. Want to join us?   _____
9. Matter much if I go?   _____
10. Sleep too long?   _____

Part VI: *going to, want to, have to*

(a)	It's **going to** rain.	*gonna*	Notice the special reductions for these verbs:
(b)	I **want to** know more.	*wanna*	going to → *gonna* want to → *wanna* have to → *hafta*
(c)	We **have to** leave.	*hafta*	These reductions are very common in spoken English.

Exercise 19

Part A: Listen to the following sentences:

1. I have to wait.
2. Do you want to come?
3. She's never going to know.
4. Are they going to see me?
5. Why do you have to say that?
6. It's never going to be the same.
7. Are you going to want to come?
8. Why do you have to be like that?

Part B: Close your book. You will hear these sentences spoken quickly. Repeat them with slow pronunciation.

Part VII: Reductions for and/or

			Note the reductions for "and" and "or." Because the sounds are so short, they might be confused or not heard at all.
(a)	Do you drink coffee or tea?	coffee 'r tea	
(b)	It's stop and go traffic.	stop 'n go	
(c)	Shall we walk or drive?	walk 'r drive	
(d)	Come and look.	come 'n look	

Note: In relaxed speech, many speakers reduce "than" to 'n, e.g. "It's *more'n* I get." This is not to be confused with "and."

Exercise 20

PART A: Listen to the following sentences:

1.   Are they coming or going?
2.   Will you pass me the cream and sugar?
3.   She's coming around five or six.
4.   I just need to run in and out.
5.   Is your answer yes or no?
6.   It's a life and death* situation.

PART B: Close your book. You will hear the above sentences spoken quickly. Repeat them with slow pronunciation.

Exercise 21

Circle the word you hear:

1.   and   or   4.   and   or

2.   and   or   5.   and   or

3.   and   or

Check your answers.

6.   and   or   9.   and   or

7.   and   or   10.   and   or

8.   and   or

*life and death = serious

Exercise 22: Short Conversation (and/or)

Fill in the blanks with the words you hear:

A: Will that be cash _____ charge?

B: Cash—wait, I mean check.

A: Do you have a driver's license _____ other identification?

B: How about a driver's license _____ passport?

A: One _____ the other is OK.

B: Here you are.

Exercise 23: Short Conversations (Review)

Fill in the blanks with the words you hear:

1. A: _____ another helping*?

    B: I couldn't eat another _____.

2. A: _____ they _____?

    B: _____.

3. A: Now _____ happier.

    B: It _____.

4. A: What are _____weekend?

    B: _____.

5. A: What do _____about that?

    B: I'm not _____anything.

6. A: A hamburger _____ shake.

    B: _____ here _____ to go?

Check your answers.

7. A: I love _____.

    B: Thanks. I got it _____.

8. A: I'm having trouble _____.

    B: I know a _____.

*helping = more food

"Care for another helping?"
  "I couldn't eat another bite."

9.   *A:* _____ take checks?

   B: Yes. Is all the information _____?

10.   *A:* _____ look _____.

   B: I just woke up from a _____.

11.   *A:* _____.

   B: I'll _____ later.

12.   *A:* Did your _____ get here?

   B: Uh huh. A _____ so ago.

2 Introduction to Linking

Part I: Linking with Vowels

(a)	How much is it?	How *muh chih zit*?	In usual speech, English has a consonant-vowel (CV) pattern. When a word begins with a vowel, the consonant(s) from the word before is moved over. This is called **linking.** Notice that a lot of linking occurs with little words beginning with vowels: of, on, I in, it, and so on. This makes them hard to hear.
(b)	She's on the phone.	She *zahn* the phone.	
(c)	Am I late?	*Mi* late?	Sometimes, as in (c), (d), (e) and (f), the beginning of the first word is dropped.
(d)	If it's time, I'll go.	*Fits* time	
(e)	Does it work?	*Zit* work?	Note that (e) and (f) have the same pronunciation. The meaning is recognized from the grammar.
(f)	Is it ready yet?	*Zit* ready yet?	

Exercise 1

Connect the words that are linked:

1. Come on in.

2. Fill in this part.

3. She's on another line.

4. We're leaving in a minute.

5.   It's after nine already.

6.   These are fine.

7.   Will you answer it?

8.   They look as if they're angry.

Exercise 2 (Oral)

You will hear the following sentences spoken quickly. Repeat the first part with slow pronunciation:

1.   _____ raining out?

2.   _____ talking too fast?

3.   _____ make sense?

4.   What _____ there?

5.   _____ I had more time!

Exercise 3

Fill in the blanks with the words you hear:

1.   _____ so tired?

2.   _____ expected?

3.   _____ do that?

4.   _____, I'm coming.

5.   _____

know, the flight's on time.

Exercise 4

"Is it" and "does it" are difficult to tell apart. They are both pronounced *zit*; the meaning is recognized from the **grammar**.
   You will hear 10 sentences. Circle "Is it" or "Does it":

1.   Is it   Does it

2.   Is it   Does it

"Why am I so tired?"

3. Is it   Does it

4. Is it   Does it

5. Is it   Does it

Check your answers.

6. Is it   Does it

7. Is it   Does it

8. Is it   Does it

9. Is it   Does it

10. Is it   Does it

Part II: a/an

(a) It's a complicated one. (b) It's an easy one	"A" and "an" are a special problem. Because they are vowels, they are linked to the word before. They are very hard to hear or not heard at all.
(c) I have a little left. (some) (d) I have little left. (not much) (e) I've taken a few. (some) (f) I've taken few. (not much)	The difference can be important. Notice how the meanings change in (c)/(d) and (e)/(f).

Exercise 5

You will hear 10 sentences. Circle "yes" if you hear an article and "no" if not:

1. yes   no

2. yes   no

3. yes   no

4. yes   no

5. yes   no

Check your answers.

6. yes   no

7. yes   no

8. yes   no

9. yes   no

10. yes   no

Exercise 6

Fill in the blanks with the words you hear:

1. _____ open the window?

2. _____ the one you called?

3. _____ that fast enough?

4. _____ it for me?

5. _____ you the one?

Check your answers.

6. _____ now.

7. _____ welcome.

8. _____, please wait.

9. _____it's free, I'll go.

10. _____, let's _____.

Exercise 7: Making Inferences

You will hear 5 sentences. After each, answer the question that follows:

1. What might the speaker be referring to?

2. Where might the speaker be?

3. Where might the speaker be?

4. What might the speaker be referring to?

5. Why might the speaker say this?

Part III: Linking Identical Consonants

(a)	been no	When the end of one word has the same sound as the beginning of the next, **linking** occurs. This is when the final sound of one word is formed but used for the following word. This makes the first word sound like half a word.
(b)	good deal	
(c)	felt tired	
(d)	Take this seat.	
(e)	More rain is expected.	Notice that (e), (f) and (g) also have consonant-vowel linking. A lot of linking can make a sentence sound very fast.
(f)	Let Tom make it.	
(g)	She gave Vick an "A" but Tom a "C".	

Exercise 8

PART A.   Listen to the following sentences. Connect the words that are linked:

1.   I wish she knew.

2.   How come Mary was absent?

3.   Let's stay late tonight.

4.   Come Monday, not Tuesday.

5.   It's somewhere near Russia.

PART B.   Close your book. You will hear the above sentences spoken quickly. Repeat them with slow pronunciation.

Exercise 9

Fill in the blanks with the words you hear:

1.   _____ later on.

2.   Come on _____ soon.

3.   I _____ people do.

4.   There's _____ problem lately.

5.   I'm staying _____ .

Exercise 10: Making Inferences

You will hear 5 sentences. After each, answer the question that follows:

1.   Where might the speaker be?

2.   How might the speaker be feeling?

3.   What might the speaker be referring to?

4.   Where might the speaker be?

5.   What might the speaker be referring to?

Exercise 11: Creating Contexts

You will hear 5 sentences. After each, suggest a possible context:

1.   Possible context:

2.   Possible context:

3.   Possible context:

4.   Possible context:

5.   Possible context:

Exercise 12: Short Conversations

Fill in the blanks with the words you hear:

1.   *A:* I got another A!

     B: That's _____!

2.   *A:* Can we leave early?

     B: _____ I'm concerned,

     _____.

3.   *A:* That job I applied for, well, I got it.

     B: I knew you would _____.

4.   *A:* This computer really _____.

     _____ me _____

     _____ to write my paper.

     B: _____ had one.

5.   *A:* This _____ mess.

     B: We'll have it cleaned up _____.

6.   *A:* Hear your building has _____

     cockroach problem.

     B: Worse _____ imagined.

Exercise 13: Conversation I

Fill in the blanks with the words you hear:

A: Think you passed _____?

B: I'm lucky _____ got a D. I don't know

_____.

A: It's not _____ get _____

_____. You can probably _____,

though. You _____ the _____

last quarter, too. And you _____ with a B.

B: Yeah, but it _____ real struggle. I doubt

_____ can do _____.

Exercise 14: Conversation II

Fill in the blanks with the words you hear:

A: We _____ down First near James, heading

toward the water. A car came _____ the

corner. I guess he didn't see _____ maybe

he _____ little drunk. Who knows!

Anyway, he _____,

missing _____ bikes by less _____

_____.

B: _____?

A: No. _____ what's more, he _____

looked back. Probably didn't _____ he'd

_____ stop sign.

B: _____ he hurt _____?

A: It wouldn't surprise _____.

Exercise 15: Sentence Paraphrase

Circle the sentence that has the same meaning as the sentence you hear:

1. a. There's some left.

   b. It's a little lift.

   c. It's a little toward the left.

2. a. It's not difficult.

   b. I feel uneasy about it.

   c. The job isn't easy.

3. a. It's a little peaceful.

    b. It's not quiet enough.

    c. I'm asking about the peace.

4. a. Datsun's an expensive car.

    b. It's an inexpensive car.

    c. That car isn't cheap.

5. a. I'm addressing her.

    b. I know the location.

    c. I have a dress.

Check your answers.

6. a. They are expected sometime.

    b. They are expecting to be late.

    c. They were sooner than I expected.

7. a. They're wrong about the time.

    b. After this time, they will be wrong.

    c. They are continually wrong.

8. a. What follows this?

    b. What sub is after this?

    c. What's after supper?

9. a. Come and bet a little.

    b. A little bid is coming.

    c. Come in a little while.

10. a. I need to pay more.

    b. There is nothing available.

    c. I can finally pay for what's available.

3 Silent h

Part I: Function Words Beginning with h

(a)	I want to **see her**.	*see-er*	**h** at the beginning of function words* is usually dropped and the word before is linked.
(b)	**She had** something to do.	*she-ad*	**h** can be dropped even when "have" is a main verb, as in (b).
(c)	Where **did he** go?	*de* *dide*	Notice the special pronunciations for "did he" and "does he" in (c) and (d). (More practice later in the chapter.)
(d)	**Does he** know about it?	*dze* *ze*	
(e)	She's **happier** now.	(not reduced)	In (e), "happier" is an adjective (content word), so it is not reduced.

*Function words include auxiliary verbs and pronouns. (See Chapter 1.)

Exercise 1

Connect the words that are linked:

1. She has given her another one.

2. Do you have any advice for him?

3. I hope he's coming.

4. I think it's sooner than he thinks.

5. Does he have any ideas?

6. I'm seeing him again soon.

7.   He had more time than he needed.

8.   Did he talk much with him?

Exercise 2

Fill in the blanks with the words you hear:

1.   Did she buy _____ pants on sale?

2.   What's _____ phone number?

3.   I'm _____ second thoughts, though.

4.   Let's go with _____ tomorrow.

5.   I think _____ pretty tired.

Check your answers.

6.   Why _____ come so early?

7.   We _____ more time than we _____ planned on.

8.   You'd better wait for _____ here.

9.   I saw it _____ desk.

10.   What if _____ says no?

Exercise 3

"Did he" and "does he" are difficult to tell apart. The difference for many native speakers is *de* versus *dze*. You will hear 8 sentences. Circle the correct answer:

1.   Does he   Did he   have an answer?

2.   Does he   Did he   know what to do?

3.   Does he   Did he   come on time?

4.   Does he   Did he   help at all?

Check your answers.

5.   Does he   Did he   call back?

6.   Does he   Did he   have a good excuse?

7. Does he   Did he   say he'd pick you up?

8. Does he   Did he   know if he can borrow it?

Part II: Questions Beginning with have/has

(a)	**Have I** explained it OK?	*a-vi*	Generally in questions beginning with "have," the **h** is dropped in fast speech.
(b)	**Have you** been sick?	*av-ya*	
(c)	**Have we** done it right?	*av-we*	
(d)	**Have they** seen it?	*av-they*	
(e)	**Have there** been any changes?	*av-there*	
(f)	**Has she** fixed the car?	*a-she*	
(g)	**Has he** stopped working?	*(a)ze*	
(h)	**Has it** happened yet?	*(a)zit*	
(i)	**Has there** been any news?	*(a)zere* *	Note the special pronunciation in (i).

*See Chapter 7 for further information.

Exercise 4

You will hear 8 sentences beginning with "have" or "has." Write the **complete** verb and subject:

1. _____ you the right one?

2. _____ enough?

3. _____ in trouble before?

4. _____ very long?

Check your answers.

5. _____ everything in good shape*?

6. _____ any new developments?

7. _____ to you?

8. _____ a problem?

*good shape = in good condition

Part III: Pronoun Summary

(a)	**Does he** know it?	*dze* *ze*	As you have seen in the previous exercises, pronouns beginning with **h** are very difficult to hear.
(b)	**Is he** coming?	*(i)ze*	"Does he," "is he," "has he," and "did he" are all very similar when reduced. Note the following:
(c)	**Has he** done enough?	*(a)ze*	does he → *ze, dze*
(d)	**Did he** come?	*de* *dide*	is he → *(i)ze* has he → *(a)ze* did he → *de, dide*
(e)	I'm waiting for **him**.	*'im*	When reduced, "him" and "them" can sound very similar. You may only hear *m*. Sometimes there is no way to tell the difference except from the context.
(f)	I'm waiting for **them**.	*'em*	
(g)	It's **his** choice.	*'iz*	"His" and "he's" have different vowels, but when spoken quickly, can be difficult to tell apart. Again, context will help you tell the difference (subject versus pronoun).
(h)	If **he's** ready, let's go.	*'ez*	
(i)	**Is she** coming?		Don't confuse (i) and (j). In (i), *sh* is not dropped, so it sounds like *i-she*. (This kind of linking is explained further in Chapter 7.)
(j)	**Is he** coming?		

Exercise 5: does he, is he, has he, did he

PART A.   Circle the correct answer:

1. does he   did he

2. has he   does he

3. Has he   Is he

4. Has he   Is he

5. Did he   Does he

6. is he   did he

Check your answers.

PART B.   Fill in the blanks with the words you hear:

7.   When _____ no?

8.   Why _____ running late?

9.   _____ any time?

10.   Why _____ the fridge*?

11.   _____ everything?

12.   When _____working nights?

Exercise 6: he's/his

You will hear 8 sentences. Circle the word you hear:

1.   he's   his

2.   he's   his

3.   he's   his

4.   he's   his

5.   he's   his

6.   he's   his

7.   he's   his

8.   he's   his

Exercise 7: him/them

You will hear 5 short conversations. Use context to choose the correct pronoun:

1.   *A:* He might not be available.

     B: I'll try contacting _____ anyway.

2.   *A:* Don't they have enough room?

     B: I haven't asked _____ yet.

*fridge = refrigerator

3. *A:* Why haven't you tried helping _____?

    B: He doesn't want me to.

4. *A:* He doesn't want any company*.

    B: That's not why you haven't visited _____.

5. *A:* I expected only you. Why so many?

    B: I couldn't tell _____ not to come.

Exercise 8: is it, has it, does it

These three phrases can all sound like *zit*. This exercise will give you more practice in telling the difference.

PART A.   Circle the correct answer:

1. Is it   Has it   Does it

2. Is it   Has it   Does it

3. Is it   Has it   Does it

4. Is it   Has it   Does it

5. Is it   Has it   Does it

Check your answers.

PART B.   Fill in the blanks with the words you hear:

6. Why _____ so long?

7. Where _____ best?

8. What _____to do with me?

9. When _____ in?

10. What _____ on top of?

*company = visitors

Exercise 9: Short Conversations (Review)

Fill in the blanks with the words you hear:

1. *A:* _____ heard anything yet?

    B: No, but _____ an appointment

    tomorrow. Maybe I'll find out more _____

    _____ then.

2. *A:* _____ to work yet?

    B: I thought I heard _____ car warming up.

3. *A:* _____ made myself clear?

    B: Perfectly.

4. *A:* _____ finished all the work?

    B: All that needs to be done for now.

5. *A:* _____ mail come yet?

    B: I just saw _____ go by.

6. *A:* The lawn needs mowing.

    B: As _____ cares.

Check your answers.

7. *A:* We're about to _____ dinner.

    B: I'm not _____. I seem to _____ an upset

    stomach.

8. *A:* _____ available later?

    B: I'm sorry. _____ booked up.*

9. *A:* Pat _____ turned in another perfect paper.

    B: I _____ studies all the time.

10. *A:* Thanks for helping _____ clean up.

    B: That's the least I could do _____.

11. *A:* I'm surprised it's priced so cheap.

    B: Prices _____ never been this low!

*booked up = no appointment time available

"The lawn needs mowing."
"As if he cares."

12.   *A:* _____ in agreement?

       B: I haven't heard _____ answer.

Exercise 10: Making Inferences

You will hear 5 sentences. After each, answer the question that follows:

1.   Why might the speaker say this?

2.   What might the speaker be referring to?

3.   Who might the speaker be referring to?

4.   Who might the speaker be?

5.   Who might the speaker be?

Exercise 11: Creating Contexts

You will hear 5 sentences. After each, suggest a possible context:

1.   Possible context:

2.   Possible context:

3.   Possible context:

4.   Possible context:

5.   Possible context:

Exercise 12: Conversation

Fill in the blanks with the words you hear:

A: How about another helping?

B: No thanks, I'm stuffed. _____ way more
_____ should have.

A: Won't _____ dessert?

B: No thanks. _____ I'd better not _____
_____ coffee either. I haven't been sleeping so well.

A: _____ been the matter?

B: I'm not sure. _____
_____ headaches.

A: _____ doctor?

B: I don't know _____
_____ for me.

A: It's _____ try.

B: I don't really like the _____
_____, though.

A: Go to mine. I'll give _____ number.

B: Well . . .

A: _____ call. _____

_____ got nothing to lose—except more sleep!

Exercise 13: Sentence Paraphrase

Choose the sentence that has the same meaning as the sentence you hear:

1. a. Where did he go?

    b. Where did she go?

    c. Why has he gone?

2. a. Outside you can help him.

    b. Please assist him.

    c. He's helping out.

3. a. What did he do?

    b. What did she do?

    c. What is done?

4. a. Has he done something?

    b. Is anything hers?

    c. Has he forgotten something?

5. a. The letter said no.

    b. They told her no.

    c. Now she knows.

Check your answers.

6. a. He doesn't have one.

    b. He has only one.

    c. He's the only one.

7. a. Let me know if he's correct.

    b. Tell him to write.

    c. Tell him he's right.

8. a. Is she thinking about a lot?

   b. Does she honor the mind?

   c. Does she mind much?

9. a. I have come to prepare.

   b. I will come prepared.

   c. I am ready.

10. a. I am waiting for his friends.

    b. He and his friends are expected.

    c. I expect her and her friends.

4 The Flap

Part I: The Flap

(a) b**utter** (b) **idi**ot	When **t** and **d** occur between vowels, they are pronounced as **flaps**. This sound is similar to a *d*, but it is much faster. The tongue tip touches the tooth-ridge very quickly.
(c) What else do you want? (d) I'm learning how to do it.	Linking makes the flap very common. Many words, when spoken in isolation, do not have flaps (e.g. "what," "to"). However, when linked, as in (c) and (d), a flap can be formed.
(e) I've **got to** go.	"got to" is pronounced as *gotta*. The **t** is a flap.
(f) Now that **ought to** do it.	"ought to" (should) is pronounced as *otta* with a flap.
(g) **title** (h) Her leg hu**rt a** lot.	Between a vowel and **l** or **r**, the **t** may sound like *d*.

Exercise 1

Listen for the flap or *d* in the following:

1.	little	6.	bitter	11.	letter
2.	bottle	7.	catalog	12.	pretty
3.	Seattle	8.	Saturday	13.	it'll
4.	water	9.	better	14.	whatever
5.	that'll	10.	idiom	15.	item

Exercise 2

Listen for the flap or *d* in the following phrases:

1.	right away	8.	go to the
2.	hot or cold	9.	not at all
3.	what'll	10.	cut it out
4.	settle down	11.	wait on
5.	what if	12.	forget it
6.	for today	13.	wait'll (wait until)
7.	what he	14.	able to

Exercise 3

Idioms can provide good practice for the flap. Listen to the following phrases:

1. better off (be in a better situation)
2. put off (delay)
3. paid off (pay the total amount)
4. get over (get well, recover)
5. out and out (absolute)
6. head on home (go)
       on out
       on over
7. tired out (very, very tired)
8. fed up (sick of)
9. get caught up (make up work you missed)
10. get it over with (do something you don't want to)
11. have had it with someone (be angry or finished with someone)
12. might as well (it's a good idea)

Listen to the following sentences. Underline the flap sounds:

1. He'd be better off in a hospital.

2. I've had it with her.

3. I paid off my car last week.

4. The doctor was amazed at how quickly he got over the flu.

5. That's an out and out lie!

6. We might as well study tonight and go to the movie tomorrow.

7. Ready to head on over?

8. Getting caught up on all this work will take weeks.

9. I'd like to get it over with as soon as possible.

10. That hike really tired us out.

11. If you keep putting off your homework, it'll never be done.

12. I'm fed up with these delays.

Exercise 4

Fill in the blanks with the words you hear:

1. That's _____ going to do.

2. He's _____.

3. I _____ compliment.

4. We _____ the full amount.

Check your answers.

5. She _____weeks ago.

6. _____ I know.

7. What _____?

8. It's _____expected.

Exercise 5: Making Inferences

You will hear 5 sentences. After each, answer the question that follows:

1. How might the speaker be feeling?

2. Why might the speaker say this?

3. What might the speaker be referring to?

4. Who might the speaker be?

5. Where might the speaker be?

Exercise 6

"What do you" and "what are you" are both pronounced *whaddaya* and the **d** is a flap. The way to tell the difference is from the grammar. Listen to the following sentences. Circle the correct answer:

1. are you   do you

2. are you   do you

3. are you   do you

4. are you   do you

5. are you   do you

6. are you   do you

7. are you   do you

8. are you   do you

Exercise 7

Fill in the blanks with the words you hear:

1. I _____ on sale.

2. He never _____ he knew.

3. He's _____ about the

    decision.

4. It does _____.

5. No way _____ do that.

Check your answers.

6. You _____ way too fast.

7. I _____ enough.

8. _____ have to say for
    yourself?

9. Let's _____ day.

10. You've _____ kidding!

Exercise 8: Making Inferences (Optional)

You will hear 5 sentences. After each, answer the question that follows:

1. Who might the speaker be?

2. Where might the speaker be?

3. What might the speaker be referring to?

4. How might the speaker be feeling?

5. How might the speaker be feeling?

Exercise 9: Creating Contexts (Optional)

You will hear 5 sentences. After each, suggest a possible context:

1. Possible context:

2. Possible context:

3. Possible context:

4. Possible context:

5. Possible context:

Exercise 10: Short Conversations

Fill in the blanks with the words you hear:

1. *A:* I've _____.

   B: _____ mean? You just
   got here.

2. *A:* _____ we're late?

   B: We won't be. I've just got one _____

   _____.

3. *A:* Where _____ hear that?

   B: He _____

   _____ the paper.

4. *A:* Could we _____ until

   _____?

   B: That would be no _____.

5. *A:* I can't tell _____ what.

   B: I'll help you sort _____.

Check your answers.

6. *A:* _____

   trying _____?

   B: We _____.

7. *A:* _____ you hear _____.

   B: You _____ job?

8. *A:* I can't seem _____ this
   cold.

   B: You'd be _____ you
   took a few days off.

"It does it automatically."

9. *A:* Did he get his _____ or _____
    _____ miss it?

    B: As luck _____, it took
    off late.

10. *A:* _____ hot today!

    B: _____!

Exercise 11: Making Inferences

You will hear 5 sentences. After each, answer the question that follows:

1. Where might the speaker be?

2. What might the speaker be doing?

3. How might the speaker be feeling?

4. Why might the speaker say this?

5. What might the speaker be doing?

Exercise 12: Dictation (Oral or Written)

1. _____.

2. _____.

3. _____.

4. _____!

5. _____.

Part II: nt Reduction

(a)	twenty	*twenny*	When **nt** occurs in a word, many speakers
(b)	county	*couny*	omit the **t** and use a flapped **n**.
(c)	identify	*idenify*	

Exercise 13

Listen to the following words:

1.	dentist	9.	quantity
2.	oriental	10.	entertainment
3.	doesn't	11.	appointment
4.	rented	12.	count on
5.	enter	13.	plenty
6.	shouldn't	14.	intermission
7.	wanted	15.	center
8.	winter	16.	mental

Exercise 14

Listen to the following sentences. Cross out the omitted sound:

1. Do you need any iden/ification?

2. Which counter is it on?

3. They planted it out in front.

4. I don't have the faintest idea.*

5. We have plenty left.

6. I meant everything I said.

Exercise 15: Short Conversations (Review)

Fill in the blanks with the words you hear:

1. *A:* Does anyone have _____
    _____?

    B: I _____ ago.

2. *A:* _____!

    B: Unfortunately we're just _____
    _____ month.

3. *A:* They don't think it's a _____.

    B: But they _____ why?

4. *A:* Does it come with a _____?

    B: _____ this price.

5. *A:* They never _____ copy of our report.

    B: That's strange. It was _____ time.

Check your answers.

6. *A:* She has a reputation for being _____.

    B: Don't _____ it.

7. *A:* If you _____ work more, you'd _____
    _____ A.

    B: I have too many other things to get _____
    _____.

*I don't have the faintest idea = I don't have any idea.

8. *A:* Who's going to _____
   while I'm gone?

   B: I'll do the honors.*

9. *A:* Looks like I found _____ too soon.

   B: I _____ to be a surprise.

10. *A:* It sounds as if your vacation was relaxing.

    B: I _____ my time in the sun.

Exercise 16: Conversation

Fill in the blanks with the words you hear:

A: You wouldn't believe _____
   I had!

B: _____?

A: I _____ for a used car. I _____ to
   pay as _____ as possible. There was this
   guy _____ me and the salesman, who
   _____ conversation.

*do the honors = volunteer to do something, meant humorously if an unpleasant
or unpopular task.

B: _____ gave you his car?!

A: _____. _____

offered to sell it—the dealer _____

_____ give him _____

_____. So, in an hour,

_____ a deal. By not

buying from the dealer, I probably _____

$700.

B: _____ that kind of luck!

Exercise 17: Sentence Paraphrase

Choose the sentence that has the same meaning as the sentence you hear:

1. a. I didn't think it was over.

    b. I still need to think about it.

    c. I already had to consider it.

2. a. He had a gray tie.

    b. He added a gray tie.

    c. He had fun.

3. a. I felt complimented.

    b. I'm considering a compliment.

    c. The compliment was very considerate.

4. a. Have you been waiting, Don?

    b. Have you waited for it?

    c. Have you been helped yet?

5. a. Please talk more quietly.

    b. You should talk louder.

    c. Don't take such a lot.

Check your answers.

6.   a. He nodded angrily.

    b. He isn't hungry.

    c. He's not upset.

7.   a. I only heard a little.

    b. It is a little hard.

    c. It hurt very little.

8.   a. Is he paying enough?

    b. Is someone paying him enough?

    c. Did he pay enough?

9.   a. I'm worried about the homework.

    b. I have the assignment.

    c. That's a sign that worries me.

10.   a. I am late due to the traffic.

    b. I'm afraid of driving in traffic.

    c. There was cotton on the road.

5 Linking with *Of*

Part I: *a/flap + a*

(a)	He's sick **of** studying.	sick*a*	"Of" is a function word (Chapter 1). Because it is a function word, it is reduced. The sound you hear is *a*.
(b)	What's the purpose **of** that?	purpose*a*	
(c)	Could I have some **of** that?	some*a*	
(d)	He's ou**t of** the office.		Remember the flap rule (Chapter 4). Notice that in (d) and (e), the sound *a* is preceded by a flap.
(e)	They have a lo**t of** money.	flap + *a*	

Exercise 1

PART A.   In the following sentences, mark where you expect to hear *a*:

1.   I'm out of time.

2.   It's sort of heavy.

3.   All of the food is gone.

4.   I'll take a little of that.

5.   It's down one flight of stairs.

6.   That looks out of place.

PART B.   Close your book. You will hear the above sentences spoken quickly. Repeat them with slow pronunciation.

Exercise 2

Same as before:

1. Isn't that a waste of money?

2. How did he manage to get kicked out of school?

3. We don't accept out-of-state checks.

4. I need a dollar's worth of change.

5. They're staying together for the sake of* the children.

6. That comment was way out of line.†

Exercise 3

Fill in the blanks with the words you hear:

1. Get _____ there.

2. We _____ gas.

3. She's in _____ budget.

4. The car went _____.

5. _____ group said they felt

    _____.

Check your answers.

6. _____ think it's a good

    idea.

7. By now it must be _____.

8. It couldn't be _____

    leather.

*sake of = benefit of
†out of line = not acceptable

9. I've only enough for a dollar's ———————————————————————— gas.

10. This meal tastes ————————————————————————

world!

Exercise 4: a/of

Decide for the following if you hear the article "a" or the reduced form "of":

1. a   of
2. a   of
3. a   of
4. a   of
5. a   of
6. a   of
7. a   of
8. a   of

Part II: Linking "of" with Vowels

(a) Most **of** us were there. (b) I hadn't thought **of** him.	Most*uv*us thought*uv*im	When "of" is linked to a vowel, the sound is *uv*.
(c) It's out **of** order.	out*uv*order out*a*order	Sometimes, as in (c), two pronunciations are common.

Exercise 5

PART A.   Listen to the following sentences:

1. What of it?
2. Who wants the rest of his?
3. That's the hardest of all.
4. We've thought of her a lot.

5. Have you heard of it?

6. First of all, I wouldn't think of asking that.

PART B.   Close your book. You will hear the above sentences spoken quickly. Repeat them with slow pronunciation.

Exercise 6

Fill in the blanks with the words you hear:

1. What _____!

2. Are you sure _____

    _____?

3. It was _____.

4. They're not at all _____.

5. She _____

    last class.

6. In _____,

    call this number.

Exercise 7: Making Inferences

You will hear 5 sentences. After each, answer the question that follows:

1. Why might the speaker say this?

2. Where might the speaker be?

3. Why might the speaker say this?

4. How might the speaker be feeling?

5. Where might the speaker be?

Exercise 8: Conversation

Fill in the blanks with the words you hear:

A: Let's go _____ the track.

B: To be honest, I'm not _____
running.

A: _____ just two _____ three times
around?

B: Hey, I'm _____ after just
_____ lap.

A: Try it this one time. I'll be _____ with you.

B: What's the _____ just once?

A: Well, you might have a _____
accomplishment . . . There's plenty _____
who feel great afterwards. And you _____
like it.

B: Look. I've only _____
before my meeting. I'm _____

_____ .

A: You sure _____

_____.

B: All right. I'll do it. But promise me one thing. _____

_____ with you today, you won't bother me

the _____ trip.

A: _____ deal. _____

won't regret it!

Part III: Past Tense Modal Reductions

			Reductions for past modals are often confused with "a" or "of." Since "have" is a function word, it is reduced and may sound like either "a" or "of," depending on whether the following word begins with a vowel or consonant sound.
(a)	You could **have** been hurt.	have → *a*	
(b)	She would **have** called.	have → *a*	
(c)	They should **have** arrived.	have → *uv*	
(d)	He might **have** accepted.	have → *uv*	
(e)	It may **have** been a mistake.	have → *a*	Notice that in (a)–(d), the preceding *d* and *t* will be flaps.
(f)	I must **have** lost it.	have → *a*	One clue that you are hearing "have" and not "a" or "of" is that the **main verb** takes the past participle form.
(g)	You had to **have** known.	have → *a*	"Had to have" is a **guess** similar to "must have" except it is even more certain or sure.
(h)	Might it **have** worked out?		Note the question forms in (h), (i), and (j).
(i)	Could he **have** come?		
(j)	Would it **have** been all right?		

Exercise 9

Listen to the following sentences. Notice the reduction of the past tense modals:

1. Could he have come any earlier?
2. That may have been true.
3. You might have told us before now.
4. It must have happened sooner.

"This meal tastes out of this world."

5. They certainly would have mentioned it.
6. I might have said that but I can't remember.
7. You had to have been there.
8. I could have sworn he said it.

Exercise 10

You will hear 8 sentences. Circle "yes" if you hear a past tense **modal** in the sentence and "no" if you hear another verb form:

1. yes   no

2. yes   no

3. yes   no

4. yes   no

Check your answers.

5. yes   no

6. yes   no

7. yes   no

8. yes   no

Exercise 11

Fill in the blanks with the words you hear:

1. That _____ true.

2. You _____ something

   right!

3. I _____ more.

4. That _____ the case.

Check your answers.

5. You _____

   angry.

6. What _____ of it?

7. How _____

   otherwise?

8. _____

   anyway?

Exercise 12: Short Conversations

Fill in the blanks with the words you hear:

1. *A:* Your accident sounds terrible.

   B: We're lucky. It _____ a

   lot worse.

2. *A:* Why isn't she here?

   B: The least she _____ is

   called.

3. *A:* I'm running _____ patience.

   B: As a _____, so am I.

4.   *A:* Can I go barefoot?

    B: You know that's _____

    question.

5.   *A:* I'm glad I was able to give you a ride.

    B: Thanks. It _____

    _____ OK if you hadn't, though.

Check your answers.

6.   *A:* Even if I _____ time, I

    _____ able to come.

    B: Well, we missed you.

7.   *A:* The costs _____ project are getting

    _____ hand.

    B: We have a ways to go before we're _____

    _____.

8.   *A:* I wish I _____

    _____ some help.

    B: What _____

    _____?

9.   *A:* It's raining. I can't finish mowing the lawn.

    B: You _____ earlier.

10.   *A:* We're _____ time.

    B: I _____.

Exercise 13: Creating Contexts

You will hear 5 sentences. After each, suggest a possible context:

1.   Possible context:

2.   Possible context:

3. Possible context:

4. Possible context:

5. Possible context:

Exercise 14: Conversation

Fill in the blanks with the words you hear:

A: Car problems again?

B: I _____ a lemon.*

    I _____ oil again.

    It _____ for

    a few weeks.

    I _____ real problems on

    the freeway.

A: I bet you _____ thought you'd be having

    this _____ trouble after only two years.

*lemon = bad car

B: It's been a real headache. I've had over $300 _____

_____ so far. I _____

_____ a _____

complaint when it first started.

A: It still might _____.

B: Maybe. In the meantime, I need a reliable mechanic.

A: Go to mine. She has a _____.

She probably _____ the

problems from the start.

B: Or told me to _____!

Exercise 15: Sentence Paraphrase

Choose the sentence that has the same meaning as the sentence you hear:

1. a. They understood the instructions.

   b. They must not have our directions.

   c. They didn't understand the instructions.

2. a. What's the purpose?

   b. What did you point at?

   c. Was that pointed?

3. a. I'll need a few hours.

   b. I'll need a few of ours.

   c. It'll take that couple hours.

4. a. It's a little shape.

   b. That shape is out.

   c. I need to exercise.

5. a. I'm not a favorite.

   b. I'm not in agreement.

   c. I'm not well-liked.

Check your answers.

6. a. You must have been uninteresting.

   b. You weren't interested.

   c. You have been boring.

7. a. We ran breathing to the left.

   b. We were left with no bread.

   c. We feel tired.

8. a. He has been sick.

   b. He has been cold.

   c. He has been in bed because he was cold.

9. a. All of the first part is dangerous.

   b. In the first place, it's dangerous.

   c. The festival is dangerous.

10. a. It depends on one's feelings about it.

    b. Opinion doesn't matter.

    c. I'm madder about the opinion.

6 Ellipsis and Assimilation

Part I: The Glottal Stop

			In Chapter 1, ellipsis, the dropping of sound(s), was introduced. In this section, you will see that a special sound, called a **glottal stop**, is used by many native speakers to replace **t**. It most often occurs when **t** is followed by the syllable, *n*.
(a)	I've been **waiting** a while.	*wai'n*	
(b)	Who hasn't **eaten** yet?	*ea'n*	
(c)	It's **getting** late.	*ge'n*	
(d)	It's **written** in English.	*wri'n*	
			A glottal stop is formed when the vocal cords close completely for a moment, stopping the air.
(e)	That's not **important**.	*impor'n*	A glottal stop can also replace a syllable as in (e) and (f).
(f)	**Something** the matter?	*su'm*	

Exercise 1

Listen to the following sentences:

1. I've **gotten** it already.
2. Pick up a **carton** of milk.
3. Are you **certain** about it?
4. I'm **getting** another one of my headaches.
5. He got a ten-year **sentence** for robbery.
6. He'd like to be a **mountain** climber full-time.
7. I'm **betting** on their being there.
8. Is it **something** I said?
9. What are you **writing**?
10. I'll only buy it if it's **cotton**.

Exercise 2

Fill in the blanks with the words you hear:

1.   *A:* This news'll _____ your day.

     B: Tell me quick.

2.   *A:* You got your hair _____.

     B: I hope it's not that obvious!

3.   *A:* Are you in the middle of _____?

     B: No. I'm just _____ here _____.

4.   *A:* It sounds like what he just said has a _____ meaning.

     B: You can say that again!*

Check your answers.

5.   *A:* It's _____ to be a habit with her.

     B: I know. And it's _____ to annoy me.

6.   *A:* Is there a _____ nearby?

     B: Over there.

7.   *A:* What a _____ thing to say.

     B: You think so? I could think of worse things.

8.   *A:* Why are you _____ them get away with that?

     B: I didn't know what else to do.

Exercise 3: Making Inferences

You will hear 5 short conversations. After each, answer the question that follows:

1.   Where might this conversation take place?

2.   What might the speakers be referring to?

*You can say that again = I agree.

3.   Who might the speakers be?

4.   Who might the speakers be referring to?

5.   Where might this conversation take place?

Part II: can/can't

(a) I can go. (b) She can dance. (c) He can drive.	I *cn* go. She *cn* dance. He *cn* drive.	In the affirmative, **can** is unstressed. The main verb is stressed.
(d) I can't go. (e) She can't dance. (f) He can't drive. (What you write)	I *can'* go. She *can'* dance. He *can'* drive. (What you hear)	In the negative form, both **can't** and the main verb are stressed. The **t** in **can't**, however, is dropped, and the final sound is pronounced as a glottal stop.

Exercise 4

Listen to the following sentences:

1.   I can't believe it.
2.   Why can't she go?
3.   Where can they be?
4.   What can I do for you?
5.   Can't she come now?
6.   I can't say enough about it.*

Exercise 5

Circle the word you hear:

1.   can   can't

2.   can   can't

3.   can   can't

4.   can   can't

5.   can   can't

Check your answers.

*I can't say enough about it = It's very good

6. can   can't

7. can   can't

8. can   can't

9. can   can't

10. can   can't

Exercise 6

Fill in the blanks with *can* or *can't*:

1. She _____ do it as you requested.

2. _____ it be done better?

3. I _____ handle more, though.

4. _____ I get there by bus?

5. _____ it wait till later?

6. You _____ ask for a nicer roommate.

Exercise 7 (Optional)

Fill in the blanks with *can* or *can't*:

1. That _____ occur anytime.

2. You _____ do better than that!

3. _____ you try it once more?

4. _____ I get it half price?

5. I _____ get it right.

6. _____ you hold on?

Exercise 8: Short Conversations

Fill in the blanks with the words you hear:

1.   A: Did we miss Bob?

     B: _____ been here
        already.

2.   A: Read any good books lately?

     B: I _____ to find the time.

3.   A: _____
        any other way?

     B: Not that I know of.

4.   A: I _____ it ready by noon.

     B: That'll be just fine.

5.   A: We _____ we'll have some problems
        with this.

     B: I _____ how hard it's become.

Check your answers.

6.   A: Think your team will win the championship?

     B: It _____ either way.

7.   A: I really need these pants by five o'clock.

     B: I'll see _____ .

8.   A: How _____ help?

     B: You _____ the table.

9.   A: It _____ twice.

     B: You _____ too sure.

10. *A:* You look worried.

    B: I just did the bills. We _____ to make ends meet.*

Exercise 9: Dictation (Oral or Written)

1. _____ .

2. _____ .

3. _____ .

4. _____ .

5. _____ .

6. _____ ?

Exercise 10: Creating Contexts

You will hear 5 sentences. After each, suggest a possible context:

1. Possible context:

2. Possible context:

3. Possible context:

4. Possible context:

5. Possible context:

*make ends meet = have enough money to pay the bills

Part III: Assimilation with y

			Sometimes in English, when two sounds are linked, they change. *y* can change as follows:
(a)	**Don't you** know?	*don-cha*	
(b)	**Would you** mind not doing that?	*wu-ja*	$t + y = ch$ $d + y = j$ $s + y = sh$ $z + y = zh$
(c)	I **miss your** company.	*mi-shur*	
(d)	**How's your** house coming?	*how-zhur*	You will find that assimilation with *t* and *d* is far more common than with *s* and *z*.
(e) (f)	**What are you** up to? **What did you** expect?	*whachya* *whaja*	The auxiliary verb can be dropped as in (e) and (f).

Exercise 11

Listen to the following sentences. Mark the assimilation with *y*:

1.   Use your head!
2.   Nice to meet you.
3.   I can't fit you in.
4.   Didn't you find it?
5.   What are you looking at?
6.   What number did you dial?
7.   Should* you need help, just call.
8.   When's† your new job start?
9.   It's what you'd expect.
10.   Don't you have any others?

Exercise 12: Short Conversations

Fill in the blanks with the words you hear:

1.   *A:* Is the lab open tomorrow?

     B: I think so, _____ might want to check.

*should = if
†when's = when does

2. *A:* How _____ like to come Monday?

    B: _____ make it later in the week?

3. *A:* I'd better be going.

    B: _____ just got here!

4. *A:* _____ worried about the interview?

    B: Should I be?

5. *A:* _____ date?

    B: Not soon enough!

Check your answers.

6. *A:* I'm taking that job.

    B: _____ better think about it more?

7. *A:* _____ like to give it another try?

    B: No way.

8. *A:* It's not _____ inexperienced.

    B: Then why _____ consider me?

9. *A:* _____ expect?

    B: Not _____ told me would happen.

10. *A:* _____ thinking about?

    B: I'm just daydreaming.

Part IV: sts, sks, th Deletion

(a) The te**st's** tomorrow. (b) It's for touri**sts**.	*tes:s* *touris:s*	*t* in an **sts** cluster is often dropped, as in (a) and (b).
(c) He **asks** too many questions. (d) Your de**sk's** in the way.	*as:s* *des:s*	*k* in an **sks** cluster is often dropped in reduced speech.
(e) I'd give it five mo**nths**. (f) She has several stre**ngths** in that area. (g) Two fi**fths** of a gallon should do it.	*munts* *strengks* *fifs*	**th** can become a *t* or *k*, or can be dropped, as in (e), (f), or (g).

"It's not that you're inexperienced."
"Then why won't you consider me?"

Exercise 13: Short Conversations

Fill in the blanks with the words you hear:

1. *A:* How about this one?
   B: That _____ much.

2. *A:* The _____ Monday.
   B: Don't remind me.

3. *A:* How much should I buy?
   B: Not much. It _____ pretty long.

4. *A:* I swam _____ today.
   B: I'd be proud of that.

Check your answers.

5. *A:* How much material does the pattern say?
   B: _____ of a yard.

6. *A:* That's two _____ failed.
   B: Math's not my _____.

7. *A:* This _____ sour.
   B: They were better _____.

8. *A:* Are you aware of the _____?

    B: Who wouldn't be?

Exercise 14: Making Inferences (Review)

You will hear 5 sentences. After each, answer the question that follows:

1. What might the speaker be referring to?

2. Why might the speaker say this?

3. Where might the speaker be?

4. What might the speaker be referring to?

5. How might the speaker be feeling?

Exercise 15: Creating Contexts (Review)

You will hear 5 short conversations. After each, suggest a possible context:

1. Possible context:

2. Possible context:

3. Possible context:

4. Possible context:

5. Possible context:

Exercise 16: Conversation

Fill in the blanks with the words you hear:

    A: Have you _____

    _____ your taxes?

    B: No. I keep _____ 'cause I

    know I'll just _____ more.

A: I owe you a thanks. Your advice about _____

_____ invest my money _____ paid off. That stock I

_____ buy took a big drop.

B: I wish I had followed it myself. My finances have really taken

_____ these _____

_____. And just as the market* was

_____ recover . . .

A: You need the luck of my grandmother. She always _____

_____ the right time.

B: Your grandma? Are you _____?

A: Seriously. She's the most financially secure of the family. And she's

done it _____.

B: _____! To

think of all the time I've spent studying investments when maybe I

should have been _____

your grandmother!

*market = stock market

Exercise 17: Sentence Paraphrase (Can/Can't Review)

Choose the sentence that has the same meaning as the sentence you hear:

1. a. Why can't you be happy?

    b. That will make you happy.

    c. I don't think you are happy.

2. a. The teacher seems to make it interesting.

    b. The student finds it uninteresting.

    c. The student can see why it's interesting.

3. a. I will do it.

    b. I can't handle it.

    c. I will never take it on.

4. a. I'm unable to speak.

    b. It was very good.

    c. I didn't talk enough.

5. a. Don't ask your roommate.

    b. You can ask for a better roommate.

    c. Your roommate is great.

Check your answers.

6. a. Can she be absent?

    b. Why is she angry?

    c. Can't she be mad?

7. a. He is unable to do any work.

    b. Do you know if he can do some work around here?

    c. He is capable of doing some work.

8. a. You can't always get what you want.

    b. You can insist on everything you want.

    c. You can't let your sister have everything her way.

9. a. Why can't he say that?

    b. It's uncanny what he says.

    c. He won't argue.

10. a. Are we almost finished?

    b. Can this one last?

    c. Can't this one be last?

Exercise 18: TOEFL Practice

Listen to the following short conversations. Choose the correct answer:

1. a. How bright he is

    b. His poor test score

    c. His failed class

    d. His success

2. a. It's guaranteed to be less.

    b. It is for last month.

    c. The product doesn't lose its effectiveness.

    d. He guarantees it's the last one.

3. a. Go together.

    b. Meet at a later date.

    c. Get some drinks now.

    d. Get together in the summertime.

4. a. There's something wrong in the circle.

    b. He likes the seating arrangement.

    c. It's wrong to sit in a circle.

    d. The way the circle is is wrong.

5. a. Jenny is going to medical school because of her good grades.

   b. They knew Jenny's grades would get her accepted.

   c. It isn't fair that Jenny got accepted.

   d. They aren't sure if Jenny is going to medical school.

Check your answers.

6. a. If she has some medicine

   b. If she has a headache or something

   c. If she has a headache

   d. If something gave her a headache

7. a. They've been taken away to see something.

   b. They're waiting to see changes first.

   c. No changes will be made immediately.

   d. They're going to change the manager's attitude.

8. a. Talk about two important things.

   b. Discuss something.

   c. Forget something important.

   d. Talk about what he forgot.

9. a. She spent half of yesterday looking for the coat.

   b. Half of the coat was off.

   c. The coat was discounted.

   d. Half of the coats were on sale.

10. a. At least he worried.

    b. At least she's worried.

    c. She's worried at last.

    d. She has more important things to worry about.

7 Frequently Linked Consonants

Part I: Linking Similar Consonants

				Linking can also occur between two consonants that are similar but not the same.
(a)	It's just me.	*jus*-me	*t/m*	These linked consonants are often formed in similar places in the mouth.* You will see that t and d are quite frequent combinations.
(b)	She was sick.	*wa*-sick	*z/s*	
(c)	What was it?	*wha*-was	*t/w*	
(d)	Sit down.	*si*-down	*t/d*	It is not practical to memorize all the possible combinations. The best way to learn this kind of linking is to be aware that such linking does occur. The more prepared you are to listen for it, the easier it will be to recognize.
(e)	I had a bad time.	*ba*-time	*d/t*	
(f)	*Le'* me know.			Some speakers use a glottal stop when dropping the final t, as in (f)–(h).
(g)	*Wha'* was that?			
(h)	*Si'* down.			
(i)	**Is there** enough?		zere	For many speakers, **th** becomes a z when it follows z or s.
(j)	What's **that**?		zat	

*See Instructor's Manual for a more technical description of this type of linking.

Exercise 1

Here are some possible combinations. Listen to the following pairs:

1. seat belts
2. did they
3. would make
4. at this

5.	what day	12.	made me
6.	meet me	13.	need more
7.	might be	14.	could that
8.	it was	15.	get there
9.	great deal	16.	let me
10.	might mean	17.	about that
11.	left laughing	18.	give me

Exercise 2

Listen to the following sentences. Mark the linking:

1. He was sick yesterday.

2. Get rid of that.

3. Meet them in the lobby.

4. I've had it with them.

5. Let's play it by ear.*

6. As I was saying, now's not a good time.

Exercise 3 (Optional)

Same as before:

1. He brought back two of them.

2. It was done way too fast.

3. Is there anything else besides this?

4. Did you get that?

5. It's not going to happen overnight.

6. I thought she made a reservation, but she might not have.

*play it by ear = not make definite plans

Exercise 4

Fill in the blanks with the words you hear:

1. _____ hoping for better.

2. He's _____ be very long.

3. _____ time, I don't know what my plans are.

4. I _____ so.

5. _____ already?

6. How _____ corn _____ cob?

Exercise 5 (Optional)

Same as before:

1. We haven't decided what to do _____.

2. I figured you _____ late.

3. How _____ get there?

4. On second thought, that _____ pretty angry.

5. It doesn't look _____ but it is.

6. Someone _____ _____ door.

Exercise 6: Short Conversations

Fill in the blanks with the words you hear:

1. *A:* What do you _____ dinner?

   B: I'm _____ for cooking tonight. Let's order out.

2. *A:* Are eight enough?

    B: Let's _____ more just to be _____

    _____ safe side.

3. *A:* Where should I _____ groceries?

    B: The _____

    best.

4. *A:* I _____ job I interviewed for!

    B: Congratulations! But _____ as no

    surprise.

5. *A:* Could you look _____ for a sec?*

    B: _____

    moment.

Check your answers.

6. *A:* Would you recommend _____?

    B: The beginning was slow but _____

    _____ later on.

7. *A:* Look _____ delicious cake.

    B: C'mon. That's the _____ I need!

8. *A:* I'm _____ take the _____

    _____.

    B: I _____

    you.

9. *A:* _____

    me _____.

    B: Don't worry. It's _____.

*sec = second

10. *A:* What did you _____?

    B: I'm _____

       the _____ I'd hire.

Exercise 7: Making Inferences

You will hear 5 sentences. After each, answer the question that follows:

1. When might the speaker say this?

2. Where might the speaker be?

3. To what idea might the speaker say this?

4. Why might the speaker say this?

5. What might the speaker be referring to?

Exercise 8: Dictation (Oral or Written)

1. _____
   _____.

2. _____
   _____.

3. _____
   _____.

4. _____
   _____.

5. _____
   _____.

6. _____
   _____.

Part II: -ed Endings

	There are three regular past tense pronunciations:
(a) They walked͜ there. *t + th*	*t, d, id**
(b) They walk there.	Past tense endings are often hard to hear or are not heard at all because *t* and *d* are frequently linked consonants (Part I). (a)/(b), (c)/(d), and (e)/(f) are grammatically different but pronounced similarly.
(c) They played͜ tennis. *d + t*	
(d) They play tennis.	
(e) I needed͜ paper. *id + p*	
(f) I need paper.	In (e), although the final *d* is lost, an extra syllable can be heard. This is a clue to the past tense form.
(g) I studied͜ too much **last night**.	Context can help you tell the difference between "I studied" versus "I study."
(h) I study too much.	
(i) He talked͜ loudly. *t + l*	The **-s†** ending for third person singular, as in (j), is another clue to help you distinguish present from past.
(j) He talk**s** loudly.	
(k) He**'s** book**ed** their flight.	Remember that the **-ed** ending can also occur with present perfect, as in (k), or with adjectives, as in (l).
(l) He**'s** looking confus**ed** now.	

*See Appendix for past tense pronunciation rules.
†Chapter 10 will provide practice with -s endings.

Exercise 9

Circle if the verb has an -ed ending or not:

1.	yes	no	6.	yes	no
2.	yes	no	7.	yes	no
3.	yes	no	8.	yes	no
4.	yes	no	9.	yes	no
5.	yes	no	10.	yes	no

Check your answers.

"It sure is hot in here."
"What happened to our air-conditioned room?"

Exercise 10

Circle the correct verb:

1. arrives   arrived   arrive
2. plants   planted   plant
3. works   worked   work
4. cooks   cooked   cook
5. considers   considered   consider
6. considers   considered   consider
7. founds   founded   found
8. waits   waited   wait
9. plays   played   play
10. studies   studied   study

Exercise 11: Short Conversations (Review)

Fill in the blanks with the words you hear:

1. *A:* He _____ expenses?!!
   B: _____, too.
2. *A:* Jack _____ all week and still got an A
   _____ test.
   B: _____.

3. *A:* I just _____ peace and quiet.

   B: I guess they finally _____.

4. *A:* What prompted* _____?

   B: I just _____ he _____.

5. *A:* I'm enrolled in _____

   _____.

   B: Why such _____?

Check your answers.

6. *A:* She _____ and day to finish your gift.

   B: I'm _____ her kindness.

7. *A:* We really _____ company.

   B: They _____, don't they?

8. *A:* Why the change? You _____ at first.

   B: As _____ out, _____

   _____ than I thought.

9. *A:* She's _____ times now.

   B: I already _____ her by letter.

10. *A:* He's not exactly _____ the news.

    B: Hmph. You'd think he'd be _____ it.

Exercise 12: Creating Contexts

You will hear 5 short conversations. After each, suggest a possible context:

1. Possible context:

2. Possible context:

*prompted = caused

3. Possible context:

4. Possible context:

5. Possible context:

Exercise 13: Conversation I

Fill in the blanks with the words you hear:

A: What do you have _____ way of wrenches?

B: We only carry _____.

A: Twenty dollars? _____

_____ just a wrench.

B: You _____ that'll last a long time, don't

you?

A: Yes, _____

_____ spending

_____.

B: Actually, this one'll* be _____

_____. I _____

you the sale price today.

*one'll = one will

A: _____

discount are we talking about?

B: Twenty-five percent.

A: _____. I'll take it.

Exercise 14: Conversation II

Fill in the blanks with the words you hear:

A: _____ that all about? I've never seen Bob

so edgy.* _____ happen?

B: _____ I know of. But I _____

_____ mention taking a day off and he about

hit the roof.† It's _____

it's _____ week, either.

A: _____ him

at all. Maybe he's under some pressure.

B: Possibly. I _____ he wouldn't take it out

_____ .

*edgy = nervous, upset
†hit the roof = get very angry

Exercise 15: TOEFL Practice

Listen to the following short conversations. Choose the correct answer:

1. a. He can't see the clock.

   b. He can't find his tie.

   c. He doesn't have time.

   d. He doesn't see the time.

2. a. She's almost finished.

   b. She bought one.

   c. She has all the buttons.

   d. She's almost won.

3. a. It was really bad.

   b. It was worth watching.

   c. It wasn't seen.

   d. It was a war scene.

4. a. She'd give anyone a piece of chocolate.

   b. She'd like pizza and chocolate.

   c. She'd give anything but chocolate.

   d. She really wants a piece of chocolate.

5. a. What is he doing tonight?

   b. What is he planning this time?

   c. What is he doing after tonight?

   d. What is he awake for?

Check your answers.

6. a. Some meat

    b. His hair

    c. A cot

    d. An injury

7. a. Criticizing a picture

    b. Looking at some paint

    c. Painting a scene

    d. Comparing two paintings

8. a. Go play.

    b. Arrive at the airport early.

    c. Play with a safe.

    d. Attend a better play near the airport.

9. a. The party was fun.

    b. Four parts were easy.

    c. It wasn't that difficult.

    d. Part 4 wasn't difficult.

10. a. The time that school starts

    b. Doing well in school

    c. What to have when school begins

    d. Recovering from an illness

8 Focus on Function Words

Part I: Listening for Unstressed Words

	One fourth of all words written and spoken in English are: the, that, to, of, and, in, it, is, I, a*
(a) **I** tried not **to** get involved.	
(b) **If it** helps, do **it**.	Notice that 7 of the words begin with vowels. This means they will be linked to the word before. This may make them especially hard to hear.
(c) Pat woke **up at** 2:00.	
(d) Look **on the** top shelf.	
(e) Jack needs **to** be **in and out in an** hour.	Several other function words that begin with vowels are: off, on, at, up, as, if, out, an
(f) **I** got **off** late.	
(g) **Is it** screwed **in** tight enough?	The other above words ("that," "the," "to") begin with a **t** or **th**. Remember, linking with these consonants is frequent (Chapter 7), so they may be hard to hear.
(h) **The** order's ready.	
(i) You said **these** are better?	Note the pronouns: these, those, the one, the ones
(j) How do **those** work?	
(k) That's not **the one** I meant.	They are often hard for nonnative speakers to differentiate.
(l) Aren't **these the ones**?	

*From: *American English Pronunciation*, 3rd Edition. Copyright 1957 by Clifford H. Prator, Jr. and Betty Wallace Robinett. Copyright 1972 by Holt, Rinehart & Winston, Inc. Reprinted by permission of Holt, Rinehart & Winston.

Exercise 1

Fill in with the correct words:

1. _____ more like _____!

2. You won't get _____ much done, though.

3. _____ knew the answer, I wouldn't be

   here.

4. It's _____ matter of life _____ death.

5. You know _____ I needed the keys

   _____ car.

6. _____ snow, we'd miss

   school.

Check your answers.

7. He came _____ second _____

   race.

8. _____ was saying, that'll come later.

9. That's _____ best

   presents you could have given me.

10. What would you say _____ offer?

11. Hold _____ sec.

12. He's been known to do _____

    _____.

Exercise 2 (Optional)

You may have seen in the above exercise that "it" and "that" can be confusing. This exercise will give you more practice in distinguishing between the two. Circle the word you hear:

1. it   that

2. it   that

3. it   that

4. it   that

5. it   that

Check your answers.

6. it   that

7. it   that

8. it   that

9. it   that

10. it   that

Exercise 3 (Optional)

"I" and "it" can sometimes sound similar to nonnative speakers. Circle the word you hear:

1. I   it

2. I   it

3. I   it

4. I   it

Check your answers.

5. I   it

6. I   it

7. I   it

8. I   it

Exercise 4: Short Conversations (Review of "I," "it," "that")

Fill in the blanks with the words you hear:

1. *A:* What's the total?

   B: _____ to just over eight dollars.

2. *A:* _____ could use a hand with _____.

   B: Let me do _____.

3. *A:* Isn't _____ something we could carry?

   B: No. _____ looks too heavy.

4. *A:* Does the promotion include a raise?

   B: _____ remains to be seen.

5. *A:* Will _____ be done in time?

   B: I'll finish _____ first thing _____
   morning.

6. *A:* Where _____ put _____
   boxes?

   B: _____ time being, _____
   _____ hall.

Exercise 5

As you learned in Chapter 2, "a" and "an" are hard to hear. In this exercise, you will practice distinguishing among "the," "a," and "an." Circle the word you hear:

1. a   an   the

2. a   an   the

3. a   an   the

4. a   an   the

5. a   an   the

Check your answers.

6. a   an   the

7. a   an   the

8. a   an   the

9. a   an   the

10. a   an   the

Exercise 6 (Optional)

Circle the correct word:

1. he   that   a

2. a   I   he

3. a   at   as

4. an   off   on

Check your answers.

5. a   up   of

6. if   off   it

7. at   up   of

8. if   is   it

Exercise 7: Short Conversations

Fill in the blanks with the words you hear:

1. *A:* Did you hear _____ head-on crash?

    B: Yeah, it's _____ wonder no one was hurt.

2. *A:* Anything planned _____ holidays?

    B: Not _____.

    Anyway, given* _____ weather, we'll probably stay

    home.

3. *A:* We have a problem _____ there's no

    handicapped entrance.

    B: I'll _____.

4. *A:* Was anything else said?

    B: _____ gist† _____

    _____.

5. *A:* What's _____

    going alone?

    B: She's aware _____ dangers.

Check your answers.

6. *A:* _____ I knew, I wouldn't tell you.

    B: _____ you're being honest.

7. *A:* You'd think he'd know better _____

    say that.

    B: He says whatever's _____ mind.

*given = because of, considering
†gist = main idea

8. *A:* Are you going to _____
    call?

    B: I _____. I haven't

    _____ ages.

9. *A:* Why didn't _____ _____
    party?

    B: We _____ plans.

10. *A:* Can _____
    early?

    B: _____

    with the manager.

Exercise 8: Making Inferences

You will hear 6 short conversations. After each, answer the question that follows:

1. What might the speakers have done before this conversation?

2. What might the speakers be referring to?

3. How might the speakers be feeling?

4. When might this conversation take place?

5. Where might this conversation take place?

6. Why might this conversation take place?

Part II: Verb + to/Verb + -ing

	"Stop," "remember," and "forget" change their meaning depending on whether they are followed by an infinitive (to) or gerund (-ing). It's very important to listen for these sounds because the meaning can be completely misunderstood. Remember that since "to" and "-ing" are both unstressed, they may be hard to hear.
(a) He stopped to study. (b) He stopped studying.	In (a), he stopped another activity to begin studying. In (b), he finished studying.
(c) I remembered to call the doctor. (d) I remembered calling the doctor.	(c) means the person didn't forget to call the doctor, but in (d) the doctor has been called and the person is remembering or thinking about that.
(e) I forgot to place the order. (f) I forgot placing the order.	In (e), the order wasn't placed, but in (f) it was placed and the person forgot about it.

Exercise 9

Circle the sentence that has the same meaning as the sentence you hear:

1. a. Kim thought about her talk with her advisor.

    b. Kim didn't forget to talk to her advisor.

2. a. Kathy went shopping and forgot about it.

    b. Kathy didn't go shopping.

3. a. Dave began smoking.

    b. Dave doesn't smoke anymore.

4. a. Jane is thinking about her ski trip.

    b. Jane didn't forget to go skiing.

5. a. Bob didn't make an appointment.

    b. Bob made an appointment and forgot about it.

Exercise 10

Same as before:

1. a. Pat thought about his appointment with the doctor.

    b. Pat didn't forget to make an appointment.

2. a. Karen didn't pick up the groceries.

    b. Karen picked up the groceries.

3. a. Joe doesn't exercise anymore.

    b. Joe began to exercise.

4. a. George began studying.

    b. George finished studying.

5. a. Bill was thinking about the time he ordered the pizza.

    b. Bill didn't forget to order the pizza.

Part III: *our/are/or*

	These three words all sound very similar.
(a) It's **our** turn.	When reduced, "our" sounds like "are."
(b) Her kids **are** going.	"Are" is often reduced to *r*.
(c) One **or** two would do.	"Or" is often reduced to *r*.
	Native speakers can tell the difference among "our," "are," and "or" from the context.

Exercise 11

Circle the word you hear:

1. our   are   or

2. our   are   or

3.	our	are	or
4.	our	are	or
5.	our	are	or

Check your answers.

6.	our	are	or
7.	our	are	or
8.	our	are	or
9.	our	are	or
10.	our	are	or

Exercise 12: Short Conversations (Review)

Fill in the blanks with the words you hear:

1. *A:* Something's wrong _____ plug.

   B: Try _____.

2. *A:* You're not planning _____ going barefoot, are you?

   B: I do _____ time.

3. *A:* What was _____ you said?

   B: Forget it. It's not _____ important.

4. *A:* I believe _____ are _____ you
   ordered.

   B: I'm sorry but _____.

Check your answers.

5. *A:* They help out _____.

   B: _____ be kidding!

"It's our least expensive one."

6.   A: Now that* _____ . . .

B: Hold on. I've got two finals _____ .

7.   A: Isn't Jack _____

_____ project with you?

B: Beats me.† He only comes _____

meetings from _____ .

8.   A: We've hardly accomplished _____ set

out _____ .

B: My _____ we'll need _____

_____ week _____

_____ .

*now that = because now
†beats me = I have no idea.

Exercise 13: Creating Contexts

You will hear 5 short conversations. After each, suggest a possible context:

1. Possible context:

2. Possible context:

3. Possible context:

4. Possible context:

5. Possible context:

Exercise 14: Conversation

Fill in the blanks with the words you hear:

A: Are you going _____ gym?

B: Isn't _____ closed? _____
holiday.

A: No, _____. It's _____

_____ busier days. You looking

_____ excuse to _____

_____ exercising?

B: Well, I'm _____ sore. I must have

_____ muscle.

A: _____ you should

_____?

B: _____ don't have _____

till . . .

A: That's right. You _____ your new job.

B: Yeah. _____ doesn't take effect until next

month.

A: Well, I think I'll go work out.

B: Don't overdo _____.

Exercise 15: TOEFL Practice

Listen to the following short conversations. Choose the correct answer:

1. a. He is too weak.

    b. He will decide in exactly two weeks.

    c. He needs more time.

    d. He will give them a week.

2. a. The manager will let him work.

    b. The manager will hear about the job.

    c. The manager will tell him later.

    d. The manager knows about him.

3. a. He wants as few problems as possible.

   b. The trouble caused problems.

   c. The sewing didn't cause any trouble.

   d. He already was in so much trouble.

4. a. She has seen his baby already.

   b. She would like to see his baby.

   c. The baby can't see yet.

   d. She would like to see the baby grow an inch.

5. a. He should begin late.

   b. He wants permission to be late.

   c. He should be on time.

   d. He doesn't want people to wait.

Check your answers.

6. a. A later deadline is OK.

   b. He should do it another time.

   c. It's already due this week.

   d. It'll be done by another next week.

7. a. He forgot where Suzanne lives.

   b. He didn't remember Suzanne's dress.

   c. He got Suzanne's dress but forgot to bring it.

   d. He didn't remember to bring Suzanne's address.

8. a. He is crazy enough.

   b. The music makes his driving crazy.

   c. He is bothered by the noise.

   d. He thinks there's enough music.

9. a. She thinks the airfare costs $700.

   b. She doesn't think the airfare will be extra.

   c. She thinks they will fight over the airfare.

   d. She's afraid of the cost of flying.

10. a. He will set the alarm for a little longer.

    b. He will sit in just a moment.

    c. He will set it just a minute before two.

    d. He will be ready very soon.

9 Contractions

Part I: Negative Contractions

(a)	Don't mention it.	*don*	In Chapter 4, the **nt** reduction was introduced. You learned that the **t** can be dropped in negative contractions. This section will give you more practice.
(b)	He's sick, isn't he?	*isn*	
(c)	He shouldn't go there.	*shun-go* *shu' go*	Because **t** is not heard, contractions are hard to hear. One way is to listen for a slight *n* sound or glottal stop in the negative contraction. Compare (c) and (d).
(d)	He should go there.	*shu-go*	
(e)	They **won't know** it.	*wo-no*	"Won't" and "want" are often confused. Note that the vowel sounds are different (*o* versus *a*). Also, "won't" cannot be followed by "to."
(f)	They **want to know** it.	*wa-nna-no*	
(g)	She DOES have an idea.		Normally "do"/"did" are not used in affirmative sentences. However, they are when used for emphasis. Compare (g)/(h) and (i)/(j). They can sound very similar when spoken.
(h)	She doesn't have an idea.		
(i)	He DID try to reach you.		
(j)	He didn't try to reach you.		

Exercise 1

Listen to the negative contractions in the following sentences:

1. I wouldn't mind going.
2. He doesn't approve of that.

3. Why don't they just forget it?
4. I couldn't agree with you more.*
5. You won't notice the difference.
6. Don't be ridiculous.
7. He couldn't have said that.
8. The weather couldn't be better.†

Exercise 2

Circle the word you hear:

1. was   wasn't

2. should   shouldn't

3. could   couldn't

4. were   weren't

5. is   isn't

Check your answers.

6. want   won't

7. is   isn't

8. would   wouldn't

9. want   won't

10. could   couldn't

Exercise 3

Fill in the blanks with the words you hear:

1. They'll be coming over, _____ they?

2. You _____ do better, right?

3. That _____ mean I approve.

*I couldn't agree with you more = I agree completely.
†The weather couldn't be better = The weather is very nice.

4. _____ he want to come?

5. We _____ going to stay long.

Check your answers.

6. He _____ plan on marrying, _____ he?

7. They _____ have decided so quickly.

8. _____ that what he had planned?

9. You _____ know until you try.

10. They _____ going with us, are they?

Exercise 4: isn't/doesn't (Optional)

If you are having trouble hearing the difference between "isn't" and "doesn't," this exercise will give you more practice. Circle the word you hear:

1. isn't   doesn't

2. isn't   doesn't

3. isn't   doesn't

4. isn't   doesn't

5. isn't   doesn't

6. isn't   doesn't

Exercise 5: Use of do/did for Emphasis versus Contractions (Optional)

Circle the word you hear:

1. did   didn't

2. did   didn't

3. did   didn't

4. does   doesn't

Check your answers.

5. does   doesn't

6. does   doesn't

7. did   didn't

8. does   doesn't

Exercise 6: Negative Contractions in Tag Questions

Negative contractions are very common in questions with tags. Example: He isn't sick, is he?

In tag questions, the expected response agrees with the first part of the question. The correct response for the above would be "no."

Listen to the following tag questions. Decide if the verb in the first part of the question is negative or affirmative. Circle the expected response:

1. yes   no

2. yes   no

3. yes   no

4. yes   no

5. yes   no

6. yes   no

Check your answers.

7. yes   no

8. yes   no

9. yes   no

10. yes   no

11. yes   no

12. yes   no

Exercise 7: Making Inferences

You will hear 5 short conversations. After each, answer the question that follows:

1. When might this conversation take place?

2. What might the speakers be doing?

3. What might the speakers be referring to?

4. How might the speakers be feeling?

5. Where might the speakers be?

Exercise 8: Creating Contexts

You will hear 5 short conversations. After each, suggest a possible context:

1. Possible context:

2. Possible context:

3. Possible context:

4. Possible context:

5. Possible context:

Part II: Common Contractions with Personal Pronouns

(a)	**I'll** be right there.	*ahl*	All these contractions have auxiliary or modal verbs, and will be reduced. Note the reduced pronunciations.
(b)	**You'll** understand.	*yul*	
(c)	**He'll** never know.	*hil*	
(d)	**She'll** be coming later.	*shil*	
(e)	**We'll** know by then.	*wul*	
(f)	**They'll** be shocked.	*thul*	
(g)	**I'm** coming.	*ahm*	
(h)	**You're** right.	*yer*	
(i)	**We're** going to try.		"We're" has the same pronunciation as the past tense verb "were."
(j)	**They're** in a hurry.		"They're" is pronounced exactly the same as "there" or "their."

Exercise 9

Listen to the following sentences:

1. I'll believe it when I see it.
2. You'll have to do that another time.
3. We'll be leaving soon.
4. She'll have to have it looked at.
5. He'll have an answer soon.
6. They'll be right over, won't they?

Close your books. You will hear these sentences spoken quickly. Repeat them in the long, noncontracted form.

Exercise 10: Short Conversations

Fill in the blanks with the words you hear:

1. *A:* How about our visiting you next week?

   B: It looks like _____.

2. *A:* Did she have an answer yet?

   B: No, _____

   me later.

3. *A:* Is Mr. Scott available?

   B: _____

   _____.

4. *A:* I _____ sneezing.

   B: _____ my distance.

5. *A:* Are they all packed?

   B: Yeah. ____,_____ first thing

   in the morning.

Check your answers.

6. *A:* This room certainly is hot.

   B: _____!

7. *A:* _____ down with a
cold.

B: _____
getting one, too.

8. *A:* _____ it quits?

B: _____ so.

9. *A:* Would you care to order?

B: _____ with an
appetizer.

10. *A:* There's a charge?

B: You bet. _____ this for
free.

Part III: Contractions with "wh" Words

(a)	What**'ll** it be?	will	"Will" is often contracted with "wh" words: who'll when'll what'll how'll which'll where'll* Note: "wait'll" is not a contraction of "will" but the shortened form of "wait until."
(b)	Who**'ll** you get?	will	
(c)	How**'d** you do that?	did	Common contractions with "did" are: what'd when'd where'd why'd who'd how'd
(d)	When**'d** he find out?	did	
(e)	Where**'ve** you been?	have	"Have" is often contracted with "wh" words: why've where've how've who've when've what've
(f)	Who**'ve** we got?	have	

*Other contractions with "will" are: "there'll" and "one'll"

"I can't stop sneezing."
"I'll keep my distance."

Exercise 11 (Oral)

You will hear 8 sentences spoken in contracted form. Repeat them in the long, noncontracted form:

1. _____ you managed that?
2. _____ we asked so far?
3. _____ the doctor say?
4. _____ happen when they find out?
5. _____ we heard that before?
6. _____ they know when to come?
7. _____ she stay so late?
8. _____ you get the results?

Exercise 12: Short Conversations

Fill in the blanks with the words you hear. (Write the long noncontracted form.)

1. *A:* _____ arrive?

   B: A little before noon.

2. *A:* _____?

   B: I was just wondering the same thing.

3. *A:* You'd better decide _____ be better.

   B: Whichever you want is fine with me.

4. A: _____ know how to do it?

   B: I read the manual.

5. A: _____ do if it breaks?

   B: It won't.

Check your answers.

6. A: _____ been supporting themselves?

   B: It's a mystery to me.

7. A: _____

   these rumors?*

   B: Maybe they're not rumors.

8. A: _____ the tests show?

   B: I get the results day after next.

9. A: _____ get that idea?

   B: _____ matter to you?

10. A: _____ do?

    B: Not well. _____ expect?

Part IV: The "'s" Contraction

(a) What's it like?	is	"is," "does," and "has" can all be contracted to 's.
(b) What's it look like?	does	
(c) How's he been?	has	
(d) This one's ready.	is	Note that the contractions are not always formed with "wh" words, as in (d) and (e).
(e) My cold's gotten worse.	has	

*rumors = talk, stories—possibly untrue

Exercise 13: is/does/has

Circle the correct verb:

1.   is   does   has

2.   is   does   has

3.   is   does   has

4.   is   does   has

5.   is   does   has

Check your answers.

6.   is   does   has

7.   is   does   has

8.   is   does   has

9.   is   does   has

10. is   does   has

Exercise 14: Short Conversations

Fill in the blanks with the words you hear. (Write the long, non-contracted form.)

1.   *A:* _____

     guaranteed for?

     B: It has a lifetime warranty.

2.   *A:* _____

     so much controversy*?

     B: I can't figure that out.

3.   *A:* _____ a good time to meet?

     B: _____ with right now?

*controversy = argument

4. A: _____ really shocked
   me.

   B: _____ the first I've heard of it.

Check your answers.

5. A: _____ yet.

   B: That does seem odd.

6. A: _____ anyone?

   B: I guess he wants it to be a surprise.

7. A: The _____around.

   B: And my _____next week.

8. A: Do you know _____ for
   tonight?

   B: I haven't a clue.*

Part V: Contractions with it/that

(a)	It'd look great.	would	"Would," "had," and "will" are commonly contracted with "it" and "that."
(b)	It'd better rain.	had	
(c)	That'd be fine.	would	Note that 'd can represent either "would" or "had." The grammar of the sentence will indicate which verb.
(d)	That'd happened before.	had	
(e)	It'll last forever.	will	
(f)	That'll be the day!	will	

Exercise 15: It'll/It'd

Circle the contraction you hear:

1. It'll   It'd

2. It'll   It'd

3. It'll   It'd

*I haven't a clue = I don't have any idea.

4.   It'll   It'd

5.   It'll   It'd

Check your answers.

6.   It'll   It'd

7.   It'll   It'd

8.   It'll   It'd

9.   It'll   It'd

10.   It'll   It'd

Exercise 16: Short Conversations (Review)

Fill in the blanks with the words you hear:

1.   *A:* _____ like what I fixed?

     B: I think _____ better cooked.

2.   *A:* _____ to carpool with someone.

     B: _____ your best bet.

3.   *A:* _____ go?

     B: _____.

4.   *A:* Got everything you need?

     B: _____ a few minutes.

     _____ as ready as I think.

5.   *A:* _____ a little longer,

     _____?

     B: _____. _____

     have dinner—_____ cold if I don't

     hurry.

6. *A:* This _____ mess.

    B: Given the circumstances, _____

    _____ looks pretty good.

Exercise 17: Creating Contexts

You will hear 5 short conversations. After each, suggest a possible context:

1. Possible context:

2. Possible context:

3. Possible context:

4. Possible context:

5. Possible context:

Exercise 18: Conversation

Fill in the blanks with the words you hear:

A: _____ play _____

    like to see next month. I _____ the title

    but I read a great review in the paper.

B: I know which one you mean. I wish _____
been reviewed. I _____
much chance of getting tickets at this point.

A: I heard that when it played in New York, _____
_____ after opening night.

B: _____ as any surprise.
Let's give it a try anyway, though.

A: _____ the ticket office first thing in the morning.

B: Good. _____
person—which _____ by now!

Exercise 19: TOEFL Practice

Listen to the following short conversations. Choose the correct answer:

1. a. She won't try to believe him.

    b. She saw something strange.

    c. The man will never believe her again.

    d. She doesn't believe everything she sees.

2. a. She expects it is.

    b. She doesn't think so.

    c. She wouldn't have debts.

    d. She would doubt it.

3. a. He'd prefer to close it himself.

    b. He did close it.

    c. He doesn't want it closed.

    d. He didn't do it.

4. a. The man left.

    b. The man visited the woman.

    c. The woman didn't say she'd be there.

    d. The woman misunderstood the man.

5.   a. There will be no pain at all.

b. He will hurt for a short time.

c. She'll go a minute after the pain.

d. He will hear it for a minute.

Check your answers.

6.   a. He doesn't see why she needs it.

b. He will give it to her.

c. He can't find it.

d. He wants to know why.

7.   a. She hasn't given it.

b. He didn't hear her.

c. He wasn't exactly listening.

d. She isn't going to tell him.

8.   a. He won't do that.

b. He wants to do that.

c. He's dissatisfied.

d. He just won't do anything.

9.   a. Eight are ready.

b. She really wants eight.

c. She wants to be ready.

d. They need to leave at eight.

10.   a. A machine

b. Some work

c. A walk

d. Her new job

10 Endings and Beginnings

Part I: -s/-es Endings

			Listening for endings is important. Occasionally they change the meaning of a sentence. More important, if you don't hear an ending, it may be unlikely that you will produce it.
(a)	He like**s** steak.	s + s	
(b)	She'**s** shocked.	z + sh	There are 8 endings in English that carry grammatical meaning:
(c)	She wish**es she** could.	iz + sh	-ing, -ed, -en, -est, -er, -es, -s, 's
(d)	The recording**s** sure sounded good.	z + sh	The singular verb and plural noun endings:
(e)	Their demand**s** seem unreasonable.	z + s	s, z, iz*
			can be difficult to hear, especially when they are linked to an s or sh, as in (a)-(e).
(f)	He'**s** finally gott**en** to sleep.		-**s** also signals the perfect form "has." The -**en** ending gives a further clue. (See Part II.) Compare (f) and (g).
(g)	He finally got to sleep.		
(h)	The bus'**s** leaving.		It is easy to confuse "is" with the plural -**es**, as in (h) and (i). Even if you don't completely hear the verb "are," listen for an extra sound. It will be the verb.
(i)	The bus**es** are leaving.		
(j)	The doctor'**s** schedule is full.		'**s** can also have a possessive meaning, as in (j).

*See Appendix for pronunciation rules.

Exercise 1

Circle "yes" if there is an -s/-es ending on the verb and "no" if not:

1. yes   no
2. yes   no
3. yes   no
4. yes   no
5. yes   no

Check your answers.

6. yes   no
7. yes   no
8. yes   no
9. yes   no
10. yes   no

Exercise 2

Circle the correct answer: possessive(-'s), is, or plural (-es):

1. 's   is   -es
2. 's   is   -es
3. 's   is   -es
4. 's   is   -es
5. 's   is   -es

Check your answers.

6. 's   is   -es
7. 's   is   -es
8. 's   is   -es
9. 's   is   -es
10. 's   is   -es

Part II: -en Ending

(a) He broke them. (b) He's brok**en** them.	The perfect ending **-en** is sometimes hard to distinguish. Listen for an extra syllable after the verb, as in (b).
(c) He's tak**ing** French. (d) He's tak**en** French. (e) He's tak**en** French **already**.	In rapid speech, (c) and (d) can sound the same since the endings are reduced. A contextual clue, as in (e), can help you tell whether the verb is present perfect or present progressive.

Exercise 3

Circle the verb you hear:

1. got   gotten

2. spoke   spoken

3. take   taken

4. eat   eaten

Check your answers.

5. hid   hidden

6. broke   broken

7. froze   frozen

8. stole   stolen

Exercise 4

Circle "yes" if you hear an -en ending on the verb and "no" if not:

1. yes   no

2. yes   no

3. yes   no

4. yes   no

Check your answers.

5. yes   no

6. yes   no

7. yes   no

8. yes   no

Part III: Adjective Endings

(a) That's a troubl**ing** idea. (b) The wool**en** one will be warmer. (c) It's a complicat**ed** problem.	Adjectives can end in: -ing, -en, -ed, -y
(d) It's **rainy** out. (e) It's **raining** out.	Notice the difference in (d) and (e): (d) is an adjective while (e) is a verb. **-y** and **-ing** can be especially difficult to distinguish because they are often preceded by the same verb ("be").

Exercise 5

Choose the correct adjective ending:

1. -en   -ed   -ing

2. -en   -ed   -ing

3. -en   -ed   -ing

4. -en   -ed   -ing

Check your answers.

5. -en   -ed   -ing

6. -en   -ed   -ing

7. -en   -ed   -ing

8. -en   -ed   -ing

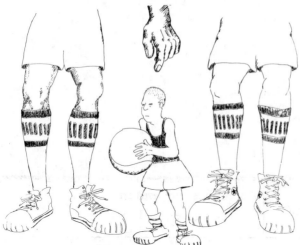

"You're a little unqualified for this."

Exercise 6

Circle the word you hear:

1. rusty   rusting
2. cloudy   clouding
3. sleepy   sleeping
4. rainy   raining
5. lazy   lazing

Check your answers.

6. curly   curling
7. snowy   snowing
8. smoky   smoking
9. risky   risking
10. sunny   sunning

Exercise 7: Making Inferences

You will hear 5 sentences. After each, answer the question that follows:

1. Who might the speaker be talking to?

2. Why might someone say this?

3. Where might the speaker be?

4. Who might the speaker be?

5. What might the speaker be doing?

Part IV: Comparison Endings

(a) It's ugli**er than** the others.	The comparative endings **-er** and **-est** are often confused or sometimes not heard at all. Usually **-er** is accompanied by a "than" in the sentence as in (a).
(b) It's **the uglier** of the two. (c) **The longer** you wait, the less chance you have.	Note, however, that "than" is not always necessary, as in (b) and (c). The meaning in (c) is cause/effect: "If you wait a long time, you will have less chance."
(d) He's the old**er** of the two. (e) He's the old**est** of the three.	**-er** and **-est** can sound very similar. Compare (d) and (e). Note that "the" is not always a clue to the superlative form.
(f) Sales have never been strong. (g) Sales have never been strong**er**.	The -er ending can change the entire meaning of a sentence. In (f), sales are weak. In (g), however, sales are excellent. Sales in (g) are being compared to all other sales before. They are the strongest they have ever been.
(h) He began working hard**er** and hard**er**.	The **-er** ending can also be used for emphasis, as in (h).
(i) It's not as hard as that. (j) Your guess is as good as mine.	"as . . . as" is a common comparative structure. The vowels will be linked to the words before, so it may be hard to recognize.

Exercise 8

Circle the word you hear:

1. long   longer   longest

2. big   bigger   biggest

3. great   greater   greatest

4. strong   stronger   strongest

5. late   later   latest

Check your answers.

6. fast   faster   fastest

7. soon   sooner   soonest

8. close   closer   closest

9. long   longer   longest

10. hard   harder   hardest

Exercise 9: Negative Comparisons

This exercise will practice negative comparisons. Choose the sentence that has the same meaning as the sentence you hear:

1. a. It is cheap.

    b. It isn't cheap.

2. a. Prices are low.

    b. Prices aren't low.

3. a. The baby is happy.

    b. The baby isn't happy.

4. a. She is lucky.

    b. She isn't lucky.

5. a. I feel safe.

    b. I don't feel safe.

Exercise 10

Same as before:

1. a. He is friendly.

   b. He isn't friendly.

2. a. There is a great need.

   b. There isn't a great need.

3. a. Nothing is simple.

   b. That is simple.

4. a. It is very easy.

   b. It will not be easy.

5. a. It's harder than I thought.

   b. It's what I expected.

Exercise 11: Creating Contexts

You will hear 6 sentences. After each, suggest a possible context:

1. Possible context:

2. Possible context:

3. Possible context:

4. Possible context:

5. Possible context:

6. Possible context:

Part V: -teen/-ty

(a)	thirteen people	thir TEEN	The way to tell the difference between **-ty** and **-teen** is by the stress.
(b)	thirty people	THIR ty	
(c)	eighteen dollars	eigh TEEN	With **-teen**, the second part of the word is strong.
(d)	eighty dollars	EIGH ty	With **-ty**, the first part of the word is strong.

Exercise 12

Circle the ending you hear:

1. -ty   -teen
2. -ty   -teen
3. -ty   -teen
4. -ty   -teen
5. -ty   -teen
6. -ty   -teen
7. -ty   -teen
8. -ty   -teen

Exercise 13

Write the number you hear:

1. _____
2. _____
3. _____
4. _____
5. _____

Check your answers.

6. _____
7. _____
8. _____
9. _____
10. _____

Exercise 14

You will hear 6 short conversations. Circle the number you hear:

1. 16   60   4. 13   30

2. 15   50   5. 18   80

3. 17   70   6. 14   40

Part VI: Prefixes

(a) They're being **irresponsible**. (b) They're being responsible. (c) Act **in**formal. (d) Act formal.	In Chapter 1 you learned that unstressed syllables are reduced. Since prefixes are unstressed, they can often be hard for nonnative speakers to hear. You may just hear an extra sound instead of the exact sounds in the prefix.
(e) I feel **uneasy**. (f) It's **an easy** one. (g) It's **unfair**. (h) They're having **an affair**. (i) She's acting **unnatural**. (j) She's **a natural** for that part.	Notice the similarity of the underlined words in (e)/(f), (g)/(h), and (i)/(j). Use the grammar of the sentence to determine if it is an article/noun combination or an adjective.

Exercise 15

Circle the word you hear:

1. clear   unclear

2. replaceable   irreplaceable

3. common   uncommon

4. comfortable   uncomfortable

5. real   unreal

Check your answers.

6. logical   illogical

7. regular   irregular

8. convenient   inconvenient

9. complete   incomplete

10. skilled   unskilled

Exercise 16: Short Conversations

Fill in the blanks with the words you hear:

1. *A:* It's not _____ matter.

   B: That goes without saying.*

2. *A:* Will it be casual?

   B: The invitation said _____.

3. *A:* Think this's something they _____ of?

   B: You got me.†

4. *A:* How do you know you didn't get the job?

   B: He _____ let me know.

5. *A:* My work load's getting _____.

   B: We all thought you had it easy.

Exercise 17: Making Inferences

You will hear 5 sentences. After each, answer the question that follows:

1. What might the speaker be doing?

*That goes without saying = It's clear
†You got me = I don't know

2. Who might the speaker be?

3. Where might the speaker be?

4. What kind of situation might the speaker be referring to?

5. Who might the speaker be?

Exercise 18: Short Conversations (Review)

Fill in the blanks with the words you hear:

1. *A:* I'm overwhelmed _____ course work.

   B: It's not going to get _____.

2. *A:* How are those _____?

   B: I haven't _____.

3. *A:* You couldn't have _____

   _____ subject.

   B: I _____ credits, though.

4. *A:* You're the only one who hasn't _____

   yet.

   B: _____ the case, I'd better get to it.

Check your answers.

5. *A:* It _____.

   B: Before you know it, _____here.

6. *A:* I need to get our bank account _____.

   B: I _____ with you more.

7. *A:* I have a _____headache.

   B: The _____ on the counter.

8. *A:* You've got circles under your eyes.

   B: I'm _____ no matter how much rest I get.

Exercise 19: Creating Contexts

You will hear 5 short conversations. After each, suggest a possible context:

1.   Possible context:

2.   Possible context:

3.   Possible context:

4.   Possible context:

5.   Possible context:

Exercise 20: Conversation

Fill in the blanks with the words you hear:

A: _____ to a

movie tonight?

B: _____ just stay home? _____

_____ to go out. Besides, this

_____ too good to put down. Would there be anything

wrong with _____ the weekend?

A: _____ be

here, 'member?

B: _____ only if a reservation _____.

A: _____ the past.

    I _____ get _____

    _____ this weather. They say it _____

    _____ at the ocean. We've had nonstop rain

    _____.

B: Well, let's hope _____ cancellation.

A: _____ my _____.

Exercise 21: TOEFL Practice

Listen to the following short conversations. Choose the correct answer:

1.   a. Size 40 is the biggest size.

    b. They only come in size 14.

    c. They don't have her size.

    d. Size 14 is larger than what they come in.

2.   a. She wishes she felt better.

    b. She never feels good.

    c. She felt better before.

    d. She feels great.

3.   a. He isn't really busy.

    b. Half-time work keeps him very busy.

    c. He only has part-time workers.

    d. He's the only part-time worker.

4.   a. It's usually quiet.

    b. It's quite usual.

    c. It's quieter than usual.

    d. The quiet is normal.

5. a. The test was short.

    b. It was a lengthy exam.

    c. She didn't see the longer test.

    d. Neither of the exams was long.

Check your answers.

6. a. Tuesday will be too late

    b. No later than Thursday

    c. Anytime before Tuesday

    d. Sometime late Thursday

7. a. Unless she eats, she will be sick.

    b. She ought not to eat.

    c. She shouldn't eat so little.

    d. She ate too much.

8. a. It wasn't so bad.

    b. That day was the worst.

    c. These days were longer than he expected.

    d. He's never had such a bad day.

9. a. They are being polite.

    b. They are talking too loud.

    c. They shouldn't whisper.

    d. They should speak louder.

10. a. She should have a harder teacher.

    b. It's difficult to select teachers.

    c. The teacher is difficult.

    d. She couldn't choose a teacher herself.

11 Special Aspects of Intonation and Stress

Part I: Statements as Questions

(a) I should do it?	Not all questions begin with "wh" words or subject-verb inversion.
(b) You got there OK?	A rising intonation at the end of a sentence will indicate that it is a question rather
(c) He doesn't want to?	than a statement.
(d) Done with it?	Note that the auxiliary verb and subject can
(e) Like it at all?	be dropped, as in (d) and (e).

Exercise 1

Listen to the following sentences. Indicate whether the intonation is rising or falling by punctuating the sentence with a period or a question mark:

1. No sleep last night
2. You had little trouble then
3. I can handle it
4. He locked his keys in the car
5. It's probably for Wednesday
6. They're finished with all they were doing
7. It won't be ready at eight
8. She thinks she's right

Exercise 2

Circle whether you hear a statement or question:

1. statement   question

2. statement   question

3. statement   question

4. statement   question

5. statement   question

6. statement   question

7. statement   question

8. statement   question

Part II: Tag Questions

(a) You got it, didn't you? ⤴ You got it, didn't you? ⤵ (b) She isn't ready, is she? ⤴ She isn't ready, is she? ⤵	The intonation of a tag question can change the meaning. Rising intonation indicates uncertainty, while falling intonation indicates certainty.
(c) You got another E, did you? ⤴ (I expected you to get an E.) (d) He's finally finished, has he? ⤴ (I can't believe he's finished.)	Tag questions can indicate sarcasm when both parts of the question are affirmative.

Exercise 3

Circle whether the meaning of the sentence you hear is certain or uncertain:

1. certain   uncertain   4. certain   uncertain

2. certain   uncertain   5. certain   uncertain

3. certain   uncertain   6. certain   uncertain

Part III: Talking To versus Talking About

(a) Did she divorce, Billy?	Intonation is very important in distinguishing the meaning of the pairs of sentences. In (a) and (c), the person is being spoken to directly. In (b) and (d), the person in the sentence is being spoken about.
(b) Did she divorce Billy?	
(c) How much did you give, Bob?	
(d) How much did you give Bob?	

*The first parts of (a) and (c) have different intonations because of question type: (a) is a yes/no question (rising intonation), while (c) is a "wh" question (falling intonation).

Exercise 4

Listen to the following sentences. Insert commas where necessary to indicate whether talking to or talking about:

1. Are you lecturing Sue?

2. Did it sting Jack?

3. Who's leading Kim?

4. It's fun to visit Jim.

5. Why did you watch Dan?

6. How did you hear Nancy?

Exercise 5

Circle the sentence that has the same meaning as the sentence you hear:

1. a. Tom is being washed.

   b. Tom is washing.

2. a. Linda received money.

   b. Linda gave money.

3. a. Fred hates something.

   b. Some people dislike Fred.

4. a. Sue is being divorced.

   b. Sue is going to depart.

5. a. It's not easy to know.

   b. It's difficult to talk to Jake.

"It's over our heads."

Exercise 6 (Optional)

Same as before:

1. a. Something is difficult to like.

    b. People don't like Sam.

2. a. It's not boring to watch Scott.

    b. This is interesting, Scott.

3. a. They are studying something.

    b. Bob is being studied.

4. a. Will someone visit Billy?

    b. Will Billy visit?

5. a. I like that.

    b. I like Sara.

Exercise 7: Creating Contexts

You will hear 5 sentences. After each, suggest a possible context:

1. Possible context:

2. Possible context:

3. Possible context:

4. Possible context:

5. Possible context:

Part IV: Contrastive Stress

	Stress on different words can show contrast.
(a) He CALLED yesterday.	In (a), the emphasis is on **called**, rather than another action such as coming in person.
(b) HE called yesterday.	
(c) He called YESTERDAY.	In (b), **he**, instead of someone else, called.
	In (c) he called **yesterday**, not another day.
(d) He never goes in DARKrooms.	Stress can also indicate the difference between a compound noun and an adjective/noun combination. (d) refers to a special room for photography. In (e), the room is simply dark.
(e) He never goes in dark ROOMS.	
(f) Watch out for the YELLOW jacket!	When the first word is stressed, it's a **compound noun**. Stress on the second word indicates an **adjective-noun** combination.
(g) Put on your yellow JACKET.	

Exercise 8

Listen to the following groups of sentences. Underline the words that are emphasized. Discuss the meanings:

1. a. He's in the library?

   b. He's in the library?

2. a. I'm opposed to that idea.

   b. I'm opposed to that idea.

3. a. You should see what he did.

   b. You should see what he did.

   c. You should see what he did.

4. a. That can be finished in a day.

    b. That can be finished in a day.

    c. That can be finished in a day.

5. a. We asked when he could come.

    b. We asked when he could come.

    c. We asked when he could come.

    d. We asked when he could come.

6. a. He said it's on your right.

    b. He said it's on your right.

    c. He said it's on your right.

    d. He said it's on your right.

Exercise 9

Listen to the following pairs of sentences. Decide the difference in meaning:

1. a. Winning will be a LONG shot.
    b. That certainly was a long SHOT.

2. a. Keep it warm on the HOT plate.
    b. Watch out for the hot PLATE!

3. a. You should hang up your wet SUIT.
    b. You should hang up your WET suit.

4. a. That's a high LIGHT up there.
    b. It was the HIGHlight of my week.

5. a. It's posted on the WHITE board.
    b. It's posted on the white BOARD.

6. a. I only read HARDcovers.
    b. That was a hard COVER to design.

Part V: Indicating Surprise with Yes/No Questions

(a) Hasn't she grown! (She has grown a lot.) (b) Hasn't she grown? (c) Was that great! (That was great.) (d) Was that great?	A falling intonation as in (a) and (c) indicates surprise, whereas a rising intonation, as in (b) and (d), indicates a question.

Exercise 10

Circle the sentence that has the same meaning as the sentence you hear:

1. a. She acted strange.

   b. Was she acting strange?

2. a. It is ugly.

   b. Is it ugly?

3. a. Have we ever had fun?

   b. We had fun.

4. a. The test is difficult.

   b. Is the test difficult?

Check your answers.

5. a. It will be uninteresting.

   b. Will it be uninteresting?

6. a. It's old.

   b. Is it old?

7. a. Is it good?

   b. It is good.

8. a. Do you think I ate too much?

   b. I ate too much.

Part VI: Using Rhetorical Questions to Indicate Sarcasm

(a) You call **that** good work? (It's not good work.)	One way native speakers indicate sarcasm is through **rhetorical questions**. These are questions where an answer is not expected. They are more like statements.
(b) **How many times** did I tell you that? (I told you many times already.)	
(c) What do **you** know about it? (You don't know anything.)	When being sarcastic, the speaker often gives function words stress. Additionally, the sentences are usually spoken more slowly and carefully.
(d) Who cares about **that**? (Nobody cares.)	
(e) Isn't this great? (f) Isn't this **great**! (This isn't great.)	When spoken with stress and falling intonation, yes/no questions can sound sarcastic. Compare (e) and (f).

Note: Sarcasm is very complex. Different aspects of stress, intonation, and vocabulary combine to create sarcastic tone. This section addresses only one aspect of sarcasm.

Exercise 11

Listen to the following pairs of sentences. Can you tell the difference in meaning?

1. Is **that** a good reason?
   Is that a good reason?
2. Can't you think of anything better?
   Can't you think of **anything better**?
3. Is **that** the **only** way to do it?
   Is that the only way to do it?
4. Didn't I already tell you?
   Didn't I already tell you?
5. Who would say that?
   Who would **say that**?
6. Isn't that too bad?
   Isn't that too bad?

Exercise 12: Sentence Paraphrase

Choose the sentence that has the same meaning as the sentence you hear:

1. a. You settled it.

   b. Is it solved?

   c. It got solved.

2. a. Have you done enough?

    b. Don't do anything more.

    c. Why haven't you done it?

3. a. What did you wear last night?

    b. I'm shocked at where you were last night.

    c. You were there last night.

4. a. Wasn't he worried?

    b. Did he cause Karen concern?

    c. Why didn't he worry?

5. a. This isn't fun.

    b. I'm having a good time.

    c. This is great fun.

6. a. It certainly sounds cheap.

    b. The sound does seem really cheap.

    c. I'm not sure if it sounds cheap.

Check your answers.

7. a. Should I see if they'll wait?

    b. Let someone else wait.

    c. I'll wait to see them.

8. a. Are you making honey?

    b. Are you baking honey cookies?

    c. Are you preparing dinner?

9. a. You look upset.

    b. Someone's with you.

    c. You brought something with you.

10.   a. John couldn't have been careless.

   b. John was very careless.

   c. How can they care less about John?

11.   a. The work is terrible.

   b. What is that work called?

   c. Did you call work about that?

12.   a. Can you be right?

   b. You don't do anything right.

   c. Is anything right?

Exercise 13: TOEFL Practice

Listen to the following short conversations. Choose the correct answer:

1.   a. He doesn't want it to end.

   b. He wants it to be over in an hour.

   c. He hopes it's never finished.

   d. He thinks it's boring.

2.   a. He'll skip the test.

   b. He already passed the test.

   c. He's going to pass the test.

   d. He probably won't pass the test.

3.   a. She expected less vacation.

   b. She needs less time off.

   c. She'll be sick for weeks.

   d. She has six weeks to get shoes.

4.   a. She's not sure about the time.

   b. She's certain when she should be there.

   c. She's wondering if six are enough.

   d. She's informing the man when he should be there.

5. a. He wants to know if he should talk more.

   b. He's certain he speaks too much.

   c. He talked about too many things.

   d. He's surprised that he talks a lot.

Check your answers.

6. a. The directions might help with the light.

   b. The model is right.

   c. He should look at the instructions.

   d. The part for that model is correct.

7. a. They are acquaintances.

   b. He's her brother.

   c. They are twins.

   d. Jean's his sister.

8. a. She thinks it is uninteresting.

   b. She wants to talk about bowling.

   c. She said why she isn't interested.

   d. She asks why it is boring.

9. a. A secret

   b. A building

   c. High prices

   d. Company lies

10. a. The man is wondering why she knows.

    b. The woman knows a lot.

    c. The woman doesn't know much.

    d. The man is confused.

12 TOEFL Practice I

Part I: Sentence Paraphrase

Choose the sentence that has the same meaning as the sentence you hear:

1. a. How did the interview go?

    b. What is his inner view?

    c. Why did he do the interview?

    d. Did he do the interview?

2. a. When are you doing the homework?

    b. When are the men doing the sign?

    c. When do we turn in the homework?

    d. What assignment are you doing?

3. a. Will they pay for us?

    b. Will they pay her?

    c. Will they wait to pay?

    d. Will they pay anyway?

4. a. May I be an assistant?

    b. Can I help you?

    c. I might be an assistant.

    d. Maybe I will assist you.

5. a. Where are you living?

   b. Why are you leaving?

   c. When are they departing?

   d. At what time are you leaving?

Check your answers.

6. a. The magnifier is near the check.

   b. I don't want to pay cash.

   c. Check what I write.

   d. I don't mind being right about the check.

7. a. I think the store is run-down.

   b. I have to run around the store.

   c. I need to go shopping.

   d. I want to run the store.

8. a. I should call someone downstairs.

   b. I shouldn't call anyone else.

   c. All of us should be downstairs.

   d. I'll be downstairs if there's a phone call.

9. a. It's about 50 miles away.

   b. It's 15 miles from town.

   c. It's somewhere in the 50-mile town.

   d. It's a sum of 15 miles.

10. a. Were you surrounded?

    b. Were you alone?

    c. Was anyone on the ground?

    d. Was anything else around?

Check your answers.

11.   a. What does she like?

      b. What does he like to see?

      c. What's his personality like?

      d. What is she like?

12.   a. I had it in mine.

      b. I'm adding to mine.

      c. What you have belongs to me.

      d. That's what I was planning.

13.   a. The price is cheap.

      b. The price has never been lowered.

      c. The price has been lower.

      d. The price is never low.

14.   a. The trouble won't end.

      b. The trouble is inside.

      c. The trouble is ending.

      d. The snow in sight means trouble.

15.   a. I had two thoughts about it.

      b. I thought twice about the ad.

      c. I'll make you think two times.

      d. I gave it more thought.

Check your answers.

16.   a. We always get asked for wire.

      b. Why do they always ask us?

      c. Why were we asked for one?

      d. They always get to ask us.

17. a. He completed work for the aged and sick.

   b. His work was finished in 1866.

   c. He finished the work when he was in his sixties.

   d. He worked for 66 years.

18. a. Is it final now?

   b. It's final for now.

   c. It's fine now.

   d. It's for a final.

19. a. Jan collected the papers before handing them back.

   b. Jan returned the papers ungraded.

   c. Jan gave the papers a grade.

   d. Jan has a handy collection of papers.

20. a. There is snow on the ground.

   b. It's sticky in the snow.

   c. I know it's sticky.

   d. I'm stuck in the snow.

Check your answers.

21. a. Let's see if it's out of order.

   b. I have to take an order out tonight.

   c. Let's not cook dinner tonight.

   d. It's out of order tonight.

22. a. We don't know yet.

   b. Don't tell me so early.

   c. I told them too early. ,

   d. He told Ellie, too.

23. a. I really agree.

     b. Please say it again.

     c. You can't say that.

     d. Can you say that again?

24. a. Woody won't do it.

     b. I don't believe he would do that.

     c. There's no way to do it.

     d. There's no wait for him to do it.

25. a. What if I ever find out?

     b. What if I don't find out?

     c. What if I don't charge a fine?

     d. What happens if I don't find it?

Check your answers.

26. a. They all accepted Tom's idea.

     b. Tom had nothing new to offer.

     c. Everyone but Tom hated the idea.

     d. Tom added an idea.

27. a. Do you care if you drink after dinner?

     b. Be careful after you drink.

     c. Would you like a drink after dinner?

     d. You drank carefully after dinner.

28. a. What's she doing?

     b. Is she up at two?

     c. Was she up at two?

     d. Was it up to her?

29. a. What caused the change to happen?

  b. Do you know what's occurring for a change?

  c. Can you give me some coins?

  d. Do you have a pen and some change?

30. a. A party is planned for the day after tomorrow.

  b. There are two parties the day after next.

  c. A party of two will arrive the day after tomorrow.

  d. There will be two parties the next day.

Part II: Short Conversations

Listen to the following short conversations. Choose the correct answer:

1. a. He's not finished yet.

  b. He'll be away.

  c. He has a way to do it.

  d. He always finishes.

2. a. It will be an honor.

  b. It's time for them to go.

  c. They'll be in the way.

  d. They'll be away.

3. a. They are tired of school.

  b. They are waiting for money.

  c. The term just ended.

  d. They can't wait for their studies.

4. a. Sales could be better.

  b. Sales are great.

  c. Sales are never good.

  d. Sales need to be better.

5. a. He is unusually late.

    b. He isn't used to the time.

    c. He knows it's a little late.

    d. He has been late more than once.

Check your answers.

6. a. She can't explain her anger.

    b. She isn't upset.

    c. She is very angry.

    d. She can't tell about the upset.

7. a. He can do less work.

    b. He doesn't mind cleaning.

    c. He can lease it.

    d. He could do it, at least.

8. a. He doesn't have energy to study.

    b. He studies tires.

    c. He's tired from studying, too.

    d. He tried to do some work.

9. a. More of her classes failed.

    b. She wants to know how half the students fared.

    c. At least half the students didn't pass.

    d. She failed half her classes.

10. a. He was beginning to think about the happening.

    b. He thinks what happened was wonderful.

    c. He was beginning to wander about.

    d. He was becoming concerned.

Check your answers.

11. a. The coffee machine

    b. The guest at the coffee machine

    c. The copy machine

    d. How to use the coffee machine

12. a. Some stories about the building

    b. The trees in front of the building

    c. The number of buildings

    d. The height of the building

13. a. The hospital

    b. Bob's ear

    c. A play

    d. Their plans

14. a. The woman is smart.

    b. The woman can easily talk about the test.

    c. Her exam was shorter than his.

    d. The test was shorter than he expected.

15. a. The baby is almost a year old.

    b. The baby was a year old before.

    c. After she's a year old, you'll know it.

    d. The baby's older than a year.

Part III: Conversation

You will hear a long conversation between two people. Answer the questions that follow:

1. a. A clock

   b. A screw

   c. A refrigerator

   d. A car

2.   a. At the newspaper

    b. From a car mechanic

    c. From the other kids

    d. From her dad

3.   a. She was told to.

    b. So she could spend time with him.

    c. She got paid for it.

    d. She didn't have anything else to do.

4.   a. It cost $75 to repair.

    b. She can fix anything but that.

    c. She was able to repair it.

    d. It was outside last week.

5.   a. He couldn't fix anything.

    b. He was a newspaper reporter.

    c. He couldn't do anything without her assistance.

    d. He was very skilled at repairs.

13 TOEFL Practice II

Part I: Sentence Paraphrase

Choose the sentence that has the same meaning as the sentence you hear:

1. a. After the application, a test is required.

   b. They all made mistakes on parts of their applications.

   c. Before applying, they will have to take a test.

   d. The application requires an exam.

2. a. It's a good price for that.

   b. You'd better not buy it.

   c. You'll never buy that.

   d. I'd better not purchase it at that price.

3. a. When was I accepted?

   b. Where am I to be accepted?

   c. When am I expecting?

   d. When am I to be there?

4. a. Whatever are the problems?

   b. We can take care of any problem.

   c. We haven't ever managed that problem.

   d. Whenever we have problems, he can manage it.

5. a. I purchased it new.

   b. I purchased a new brand.

   c. I bought a new blend.

   d. I brought the new one.

Check your answers.

6. a. I didn't do it well.

   b. It didn't work.

   c. He didn't do any good.

   d. I couldn't do anything.

7. a. It's wonderful you wore it.

   b. I wondered if you were out.

   c. I'm not surprised you're tired.

   d. Don't wonder about wearing it.

8. a. It occurred in 1915.

   b. It was exactly 1952.

   c. It happened in 1950.

   d. It existed in 1915.

9. a. It was the first thing this morning.

   b. It will be done in the morning.

   c. The first thing is tomorrow morning.

   d. I'll think about it first in the morning.

10. a. A good time to call me is at work.

    b. You called at the right moment.

    c. Your call was timed.

    d. You called at the time I was walking.

Check your answers.

11.   a. How about getting hamburgers, fries, and shakes?

  b. Do you want to order food first?

  c. Let's order our food quickly.

  d. What was the first food you ordered?

12.   a. I'm sure the school was built a hundred years ago.

  b. Definitely, the school was censured.

  c. Someone had found the school a century ago.

  d. The school must have been funded for a hundred years.

13.   a. I would be happier if we didn't stay at the beach.

  b. We were happy when we stayed at the ocean.

  c. I would love to stay at the ocean.

  d. Nothing makes me happy about staying at the beach.

14.   a. This street is west of the other one.

  b. This load is worse than the others.

  c. The condition of this street is worse.

  d. The other one is worse than this.

15.   a. I like products that don't require a lot of time.

  b. That project will be a waste of time.

  c. That project won't be done in a long time.

  d. We need to spend more time on waste projects.

Check your answers.

16.   a. I realize it hurt.

  b. I know the condition of my heart.

  c. I memorized it.

  d. I know it's hard.

17. a. The price of the checks has doubled.

   b. Check the price again.

   c. It'd be better if the prize were checked.

   d. You should see if that price doubled.

18. a. They're asking for more.

   b. The price is too high.

   c. What they ask weighs too much.

   d. They had too many requests.

19. a. I heard you were sick at work.

   b. I was sick because I got tired at work.

   c. I tried to work hard when I was sick.

   d. I really want to work less.

20. a. Someone bought it from me 4 months ago.

   b. I sold it when it was 4 months old.

   c. I've been selling it for 4 months.

   d. I sewed it 4 months ago.

Check your answers.

21. a. It fits better than the other.

   b. It's OK to like others.

   c. I'd like another one.

   d. It fits OK, but not like the other.

22. a. What's the matter?

   b. What problems did you see?

   c. What's the matter with the seams?

   d. That seems to be trouble.

23. a. He's chosen to swim in the deep end.

    b. Depending on the weather and his grades, he might choose to swim.

    c. He's chosen to swim with a great team.

    d. He will be picked for the team if his grades are good.

24. a. Those things aren't available then.

    b. There are no openings for that time.

    c. I'm afraid of what's available at that time.

    d. I'm scared there will be nothing available then.

25. a. They're the parents of the other child.

    b. It's apparent that they want the other children.

    c. Obviously they want another child.

    d. Their parents want another child.

Check your answers.

26. a. That paper has the best jobs for reporters.

    b. That paper has long articles.

    c. That paper has been reporting jobs for a long time.

    d. That paper has better articles than the others.

27. a. I don't care about finishing this.

    b. I feel very careless.

    c. I could be less careless.

    d. I carelessly finished the project.

28. a. We've done more than we planned.

    b. We achieved more last year.

    c. We set our accomplishments last year.

    d. We said more about our accomplishments this past year.

29. a. I'm the only one who is cold.

b. The room is frozen.

c. Is anyone else cold?

d. Which is frozen: the room or I?

30. a. Let me have your car; however, it might be late.

b. No matter how late it is, phone me.

c. Give me a call unless it is late.

d. How can you ever call me when it is so late?

Check your answers.

Part II: Short Conversations

Listen to the following short conversations. Choose the correct answers:

1. a. They have to believe.

b. They hate to believe it.

c. They have to go.

d. They hate living there.

2. a. He'll do anything to finish.

b. He'll take his work somewhere else.

c. He'll work wherever it's necessary.

d. He'll do what takes forever.

3. a. You can't buy it.

b. It doesn't affect anything.

c. You can buy something more effective.

d. It's the best.

4. a. She will miss it.

b. She plans on attending.

c. She's supposed to go to something else wonderful.

d. She will if it's very good.

5. a. The newspaper

    b. Some math

    c. His printing

    d. An advertisement

Check your answers.

6. a. He will meet her.

    b. He will see her another way.

    c. He is doing something else.

    d. He will see her at another meeting.

7. a. He has no time to prepare it.

    b. He can have it ready quickly.

    c. He has no time to read.

    d. He is reading about time.

8. a. Maureen expected rain.

    b. The weather wasn't good.

    c. They thought there would be more.

    d. They got the mooring they wanted.

9. a. If she wants to cook

    b. If they will be able to get a cook

    c. If cooking facilities will be provided

    d. If they want to cook a chicken

10. a. Making the decision is complicated.

    b. He's involved in a process.

    c. It's a process he's not involved in.

    d. It's a system that evolved.

Check your answers.

11. a. His mind

b. The mine

c. Her note

d. A slip

12. a. They care a lot.

b. They don't care.

c. They care about no one.

d. Not one person cared.

13. a. John will quit today.

b. John got a new job today.

c. John will get a job the next day.

d. John will probably never quit his job.

14. a. He has to go home.

b. He asks if he may go home.

c. He has time.

d. He's building his house.

15. a. She isn't very hungry.

b. She hasn't eaten yet.

c. She got something for lunch.

d. She's started to eat.

Part III: Conversation

You will hear a long conversation between two people. Answer the questions that follow:

1. a. A car   c. A ticket

b. A judge   d. A meter

2. a. There's fifty minutes left on the meter.

    b. He parked on the curb.

    c. He has fifteen minutes before the meter runs out.

    d. His friend can tell distances well.

3. a. There's a penalty for being late.

    b. He might go to jail.

    c. He will have to see the judge.

    d. He will feel guilty if he doesn't.

4. a. Talk to a struggling student.

    b. Argue his case in traffic court.

    c. Pay the late fee early.

    d. Pay the ticket on time.

5. a. Get headaches.

    b. Park downtown.

    c. Find another form of transportation.

    d. Stop going downtown.

6. a. In court

    b. On the bus

    c. At a park

    d. Downtown

14 TOEFL Practice III

Part I: Sentence Paraphrase

Choose the sentence that has the same meaning as the sentence you hear:

1. a. I heard your conversation.

   b. I couldn't hear your discussion.

   c. I couldn't help the conversation.

   d. I heard everything but the conversation.

2. a. She looked at the oil level.

   b. She doesn't check the oil anymore.

   c. She'll need to examine the oil.

   d. The oil stopped after it was checked.

3. a. The bus doesn't belong.

   b. The bus is coming soon.

   c. The bus is too long.

   d. The bus should be longer.

4. a. He's excited about it.

   b. He's out of signs at the moment.

   c. He's not inside right now.

   d. He's out of sight now.

5.   a. I'm using it.

    b. I used to do it.

    c. I use it.

    d. I'm accustomed to it.

Check your answers.

6.   a. Did we see the park yesterday?

    b. Were you at the park yesterday?

    c. Did you see the park yesterday?

    d. Were you at the sea or the park yesterday?

7.   a. You accused me of leaving.

    b. You'll have to give me reasons for leaving.

    c. I'm sorry but I have to leave.

    d. You left without an excuse.

8.   a. It took a second to think about the clothes.

    b. The shirt matches those clothes.

    c. What shirt goes with those clothes?

    d. That shirt does not match that outfit.

9.   a. He was in a black mood after the question.

    b. He has to ask a question soon.

    c. He was questioned too soon about his bank.

    d. He didn't know what to say.

10.   a. He's the youngest to ever go.

    b. He's the youngest in the tent.

    c. He went far as the youngest to attend.

    d. He's not far from the youngest.

Check your answers.

11. a. She's at least worried.

    b. That isn't an important concern.

    c. She's the least worried of all.

    d. At least she's over her concerns.

12. a. I try hard to see improvement.

    b. My hard work doesn't make a difference.

    c. My eyesight doesn't seem to be improving.

    d. Improvement doesn't seem to matter.

13. a. He is very impolite.

    b. That's someone's rule.

    c. Is he rude?

    d. Have you ever seen such a root?

14. a. You'll be out this hour.

    b. You'll be on an outing for one hour.

    c. It won't take more than an hour.

    d. You'll be ill for an hour.

15. a. The plane was leaving when I got to the airport.

    b. I got to the airport just in time.

    c. I missed the plane.

    d. After I got to the airport, the plane left.

Check your answers.

16. a. It will take place at 1:30.

    b. I was held up in room 130.

    c. We'll hold it at 1:30.

    d. Go to room 130.

17. a. I want to know how to exercise.

b. Please let me know about the work.

c. Tell me what happens.

d. There's a limit to the workouts.

18. a. I have been running better lately.

b. Unless I hurry, I won't be on time.

c. I'm better at running lately.

d. I need to improve my running rate.

19. a. I couldn't agree with you anymore.

b. I couldn't be angry.

c. I can disagree with you.

d. I really agree with you.

20. a. It is obvious.

b. I went without saying anything.

c. Go and don't talk.

d. Leave without saying anymore.

Check your answers.

21. a. You know half of it.

b. You don't know much about it.

c. You don't have it.

d. You don't know if half of it fits.

22. a. She has no plans for her job during her pregnancy.

b. She won't keep on working.

c. Since she's been pregnant, she doesn't take time to do her job.

d. She will continue working in spite of her condition.

23. a. It wasn't easy to hear.

b. It was easier than I expected.

c. I couldn't hear at all.

d. It was so hard to do.

24. a. I tried waiting the whole day.

b. The wedding made me tired.

c. I don't want to wait anymore.

d. I'm tired from wading today.

25. a. Don't interfere with her writing.

b. She's writing a letter.

c. She wants to write a letter.

d. Allow her to be right.

Check your answers.

26. a. I'm afraid it's sooner than anything.

b. I'm afraid they'll test us sooner.

c. He's afraid to think about the test.

d. He's not expecting the test so soon.

27. a. I made mistakes because it was too hard.

b. I feel very hot.

c. My mistake made me feel hot.

d. I made mistakes because I'm hard of hearing.

28. a. She looks younger than she is.

b. She's not as old as you might think.

c. She's 30 years old.

d. She's not older than 30.

29. a. The competition seems equal.

    b. They will get a raise next time.

    c. They're predicting a time for the race.

    d. They're tying the lace.

30. a. Our interests are uncommon.

    b. We don't have anything considered common.

    c. We are very different.

    d. It's interesting how common we are.

Part II: Short Conversations

Listen to the following short conversations. Choose the correct answer:

1. a. It's too difficult to fix.

    b. It should be easy.

    c. It should be difficult.

    d. It shouldn't be difficult for two.

2. a. The weather is surprising.

    b. She wants to be surprised.

    c. She expects rain.

    d. She's giving a surprise whether or not it rains.

3. a. She isn't allowed to go to school.

    b. She doesn't get to go to school.

    c. She doesn't have any energy.

    d. She's going when she can.

4. a. Replacing the light globe

    b. Putting out a fire

    c. Getting a new ball

    d. Fixing a light

5.   a. Work is a pleasure.

  b. His job is stressful.

  c. Someone is with him from work.

  d. He's being pressured to work.

Check your answers.

6.   a. To an old shop

  b. To a frame shop

  c. To our shop

  d. To a shop on Sleet

7.   a. He doesn't know where Bill is.

  b. He doesn't know his age.

  c. He might be in Asia.

  d. He hasn't seen someone age so much.

8.   a. She did work all weekend.

  b. She worked in tires over the weekend.

  c. She tried to be thorough.

  d. She walked the whole weekend.

9.   a. Something strange

  b. A pretty stranger

  c. A strange knit

  d. Something strange in the earth

10.   a. Three is not safe enough.

  b. It's better to be on the side that's safe.

  c. Two may not be enough.

  d. It's better to get to a safe site.

Check your answers.

11. a. She needs to write a check for the oven.

     b. She needs a checkup.

     c. She needs to turn up the oven.

     d. She needs to see if the oven is off.

12. a. She wants a second room near the desert.

     b. She doesn't want another helping.

     c. She wants more of the main dish.

     d. She's saving her dessert.

13. a. The last thing he needs is a casserole.

     b. He doesn't want any more help.

     c. He needs another person to help.

     d. Bob will be the last person in the kitchen.

14. a. You should be very careful.

     b. It's not safe anymore.

     c. You will never be secure.

     d. There aren't two safes.

15. a. He wants to be told what he should do.

     b. He just told everybody what to do.

     c. He wants to know who did that.

     d. He would like to know everyone's duties.

Part III: Conversation

You will hear a long conversation between two people. Answer the questions that follow:

1. a. To her physics class

    b. To a lecture

    c. To the store

    d. To the doctor

2. a. An exam

    b. Some milk

    c. Some math questions

    d. Some cigarettes

3. a. She's good in math.

    b. It resembles water.

    c. She drinks it.

    d. It doesn't matter.

4. a. They both smoke.

    b. They aren't healthy.

    c. They are roommates.

    d. They like lectures.

5. a. At a store

    b. At school

    c. At a health store

    d. At home

Appendix

Past Tense Pronunciations

-**ed** is pronounced as *t* after voiceless sounds. Voiceless sounds are: *p, t, k, s, f, sh, ch, th**

-**ed** is pronounced as *d* after voiced sounds. Voiced sounds are: *b, d, g, z, v, zh, j, m, n, ng, l, r, th**

-**ed** is pronounced as *id* after **t** and **d**.

Pronunciation for -s

-**s** is pronounced as *s* after voiceless sounds, except: *s, sh, ch.*

-**s** is pronounced as *z* after voiced sounds, except: *z, zh, j.*

-**s** is pronounced as *iz* after: *s, z, sh, ch, j, zh.*

***th** has two pronunciations. The symbol for the voiceless **th** is: [Θ]. The symbol for the voiced **th** *is: [ð]*

Answer Key

Chapter 1

Exercise 3

1. Wait, weighed
2. stay, steak
3. lot, lot
4. slope, slow
5. feet, fee
6. laid, laid

Exercise 4

1. tip (yes)
2. wait (yes)
3. way (no)
4. me (no)
5. let (yes)

Exercise 5

1. meet (yes)
2. say (no)
3. had (yes)
4. may (no)
5. gray (no)

Exercise 6

1. He is sad.
2. She broke a rib.
3. I lost my bag.
4. That tastes bad.
5. Please open the lid.

Exercise 7

1. You were right.
2. Please call a cab.
3. Where's my bathrobe?
4. It's in the grocery sack.
5. I don't know where she's at. *

*informal English

Exercise 8

1. great
2. cab
3. card
4. up
5. heart

Exercise 9

1. tip
2. job
3. check
4. bit
5. birth date

Exercise 13

1. int$\not{e}$resting
2. fam$\not{i}$ly
3. fact$\not{o}$ry
4. ord$\not{i}$nary
5. s$\not{u}$ppose
6. fin$\not{a}$lly
7. veg$\not{e}$tables
8. sep$\not{a}$rate
9. ev$\not{e}$ning
10. $\not{e}$specially
11. av$\not{e}$rage
12. Flor$\not{i}$da

Exercise 14

1. gen$\not{e}$rous
2. hor$\not{r}$ible
3. cab$\not{i}$net
4. temp$\not{e}$rature
5. diff$\not{e}$rent
6. asp$\not{i}$rin
7. gas$\not{o}$line
8. g$\not{a}$rage
9. ref$\not{e}$rence
10. fav$\not{o}$rite

Exercise 15

1. trav'ler
2. mem'ry
3. 'nough
4. ev'ry
5. 'nother
6. cam'ra
7. bak'ry
8. 'stead

Exercise 17

1. Are you
2. they got
3. will
4. was/for the
5. was/than
6. the back
7. up late
8. you tried
9. were/before
10. stop that

Exercise 18

2. Do you
3. It
4. Do you remember
5. Is or Is there
6. Do you
7. Do you
8. Do you
9. Does it
10. Did you

Exercise 21

1. Does that look black and blue?
2. Were you sick or tired?
3. They'll be here sooner or later.

4. It happens time and time again.
5. This one or the other one?
6. It's more or less what she planned.
7. Did you want a shampoo and cut?
8. Two or three will do.
9. I need a few odds and ends.
10. She visits now and then.

Exercise 22

or
or
and
or

Exercise 23

1. Care for/bite
2. Were/asking for me/I believe so
3. you look/helps to talk
4. you going to do this/ Probably sleep
5. you want to do/going to do
6. and chocolate/for/or
7. your shirt/really cheap
8. with my car/garage nearby
9. Do you/up-to-date
10. You/really tired/nap
11. I want to know more/ tell you
12. family finally/week or

Chapter 2

Exercise 2

1. Is it
2. Am I
3. Does it
4. was in
5. If only

Exercise 3

1. Why am I
2. When are we
3. Did I
4. If it's OK
5. As far as I

Exercise 4

1. Does it come with anything else?
2. Is it arriving on time?
3. Is it like you thought?
4. Does it stay open late?
5. Does it help to talk?
6. Does it matter much if I go?
7. Is it something I can do?
8. Is it very cloudy out?
9. Is it what you ordered?
10. Does it need more salt?

Exercise 5

1. We're on time.
2. It's bigger than you think.
3. She's an excellent student.
4. It's a little trouble.
5. Here's another one.
6. There's a few left.
7. She's arriving any minute.
8. Here's a present for you.
9. She wants to major in architecture.
10. I think it's far away, though.

Exercise 6

1. Mind if I
2. Am I
3. Did I do
4. What's in
5. Why are
6. It's all over
7. All are
8. If I'm late
9. As long as
10. If it's OK/leave early

Exercise 7

1. It's in an ad.
2. There will be a few in a minute.
3. That's an expensive-looking car.
4. Is it big enough for you?

5. You look as if you're angry.

Exercise 9

1. Ask questions
2. over real*
3. guess some
4. been no
5. home Monday

Exercise 10

1. This section is full.
2. You are going where?
3. What time's it taking place?
4. I'm looking for one with cheaper rent.
5. It's worth the money.

Exercise 11

1. How many are ready?
2. Care for another one?
3. She's coming as early as when?
4. Am I walking too fast?
5. Even if it's late, I will accept it.

Exercise 12

1. two in a row
2. As far as/it's OK
3. all along
4. makes a difference/It took/half as long/I wish I
5. place is a/in an hour
6. a little/than I ever

Exercise 13

that test
if I/if I should drop it
going to/any easier/handle it/
were in/same mess/came out
was a/if I/it twice

Exercise 14

were riding/from around/us
or/was a/sped directly past
us/our/than an inch
Was anyone else around

*informal English

And/never even/even know/
run a
Wonder if/anyone else
me a bit

Exercise 15

1. I have a little left. (a)
2. It's an easy job. (a)
3. I'm just asking for a
   little peace and quiet.
   (b)
4. That's an expensive car.
   (c)
5. I have the address here.
   (b)
6. I'm expecting them
   sooner or later. (a)
7. Time after time, they
   were wrong. (c)
8. What's up after this? (a)
9. Come, in a little bit. (c)
10. Even if I pay more,
    there are none
    available. (b)

Chapter 3

Exercise 2

1. his
2. her
3. having
4. her
5. he's
6. has he
7. had/had
8. her
9. on her
10. he

Exercise 3

1. Does he
2. Did he
3. Did he
4. Does he
5. Did he
6. Did he
7. Did he
8. Does he

Exercise 4

1. Have I given
2. Have you seen
3. Have they been
4. Has it taken

5. Has he left
6. Have there been
7. Has she spoken
8. Has there been

Exercise 5

1. Where did he live?
2. Why has he lied?
3. Has he complained?
4. Is he complaining?
5. Does he need help?
6. Why is he outside?
7. did he say
8. has he been
9. Does he have
10. is he cleaning
11. Did he do
12. does he begin

Exercise 6

1. It's not that he's
   unfriendly.
2. I think his plans were
   changed.
3. He's determined to
   change jobs.
4. It's his only complaint.
5. What's his idea on
   this?
6. He says he's going to
   do what?
7. It's sooner than he's
   planning.
8. It's his chance to buy a
   whole 'nother one.*

Exercise 7

1. him
2. them
3. him
4. him
5. them

Exercise 8

1. Does it look like rain?
2. Has it become a
   problem recently?
3. Does it keep for long?
4. Is it really what you
   want?
5. Is it handmade?

*informal English

6. does it take
7. does it work
8. has it got
9. is it due
10. is it

Exercise 9

1. Have you/I have/from
   her
2. Have they gone/his
3. Have I
4. Have we
5. Has the/her
6. if he
7. have/hungry/have
8. Is he/He's all
9. has/think he
10. her/for her
11. have
12. Is he/his

Exercise 10

1. I wish you had been
   here sooner.
2. The price has gone up
   again.
3. I'm sure her grades are
   high.
4. How did he do on his
   exam?
5. Has there been any
   change in her
   condition?

Exercise 11

1. If only I had studied!
2. Let's pick her up in an
   hour.
3. How did he do in his
   interview?
4. My guess is he's sick.
5. If he wants more, it's
   here.

Exercise 12

I've had/than I
you have any
And/have any
Has anything
I've also been having
Have you seen a
if he could do anything
worth a
one I have
you her/Give her a/You've

Exercise 13

1. Where has he gone? (a)
2. Please help him out. (b)
3. What's he done? (a)
4. Does he have everything? (c)
5. They let her know. (c)
6. It's his only one. (b)
7. Tell me if he's right. (a)
8. Does she have much on her mind? (a)
9. I have come prepared. (c)
10. I'm expecting him and his friends in a minute. (b)

Chapter 4

Exercise 4

1. what he's
2. out in back
3. consider it a
4. paid off
5. dropped out a few
6. Not as far as
7. should I tell her about it
8. not at all what I

Exercise 5

1. I've had it!
2. Wait a while.
3. It has me worried.
4. Look it up in another book.
5. Fill it up with unleaded.

Exercise 6

1. What are you thinking about?
2. What do you think about her article?
3. What do you say to dinner tonight?
4. What are you planning for tomorrow?
5. What are you upset about?
6. What are you expecting to have happen?
7. What do you need to figure out?
8. What do you know about her?

Exercise 7

1. bought it
2. let on
3. a little bitter
4. it automatically
5. would I
6. did it again
7. had had
8. What do you
9. call it a
10. got to be

Exercise 8

1. Do you like it hot or cold?
2. Put a quarter in the meter.
3. It'll turn out better than you think.
4. What if it's too expensive?
5. He out-and-out lied about it.

Exercise 9

1. I'm plain tired out.
2. Let's check it out.
3. What do you mean the light is out?
4. He might as well be in a hospital.
5. It ought to be OK.

Exercise 10

1. got to go/What do you
2. What if/more to go
3. did he/said he read it in
4. put it off/eight or nine/ trouble at all
5. what is/it out
6. What do you say to/it again/might as well
7. Wait'll/what happened/ got a new
8. to get over/better off if
9. flight OK/did he/would have it
10. Is it ever/You said it

Exercise 11

1. We ought to head on home.
2. I think it's straight ahead.

3. I'm fed up with this job.
4. What an idiot!
5. I've got a few more to go.

Exercise 12

1. She walked away without a word.
2. What are you leaving for?
3. What if I say no?
4. Now that ought to do it!
5. I'm signed up on a waiting list.

Exercise 15

1. change for a twenty/did an hour
2. What a great apartment/ renting it another
3. good idea/didn't say
4. printer/Not at
5. got a/sent on
6. a gentle dentist/count on
7. were to/get an/caught up on
8. water the plants
9. out a little/meant it
10. spent all

Exercise 16

what a day
What happened
went looking/wanted/little
cash/waiting near/overheard
our
And he
Not exactly/But he/wasn't
about to/what he wanted/we
had ourselves/saved over
If only I could have

Exercise 17

1. I hadn't thought it over yet. (b)
2. He had a great time. (c)
3. I consider it a compliment. (a)
4. Have you been waited on yet? (c)
5. You shouldn't talk so loud. (a)
6. He's not at all angry. (c)
7. It only hurt a little. (c)

8. Is he getting paid
   enough? (b)
9. That assignment has
   me worried. (a)
10. I'm afraid I was caught
    in traffic. (a)

Chapter 5

Exercise 3

1. out of
2. ran out of
3. charge of the
4. out of control
5. Most of the/out of
   shape
6. Neither of them
7. out of date
8. made out of
9. worth of
10. out of this

Exercise 4

1. That was a waste.
2. Let's get rid of that.
3. I dropped out of the
   race after one lap.
4. He had a terrible time
   finding my house.
5. I'll have another one of
   those.
6. It's a bigger problem
   than they thought.
7. In case of fire, break
   this glass.
8. What a special way to
   celebrate!

Exercise 6

1. a waste of energy
2. about all of it
3. expected of us
4. proud of it
5. skipped out of her
6. case of an accident

Exercise 7

1. You're acting like I'm
   hard of hearing.
2. We're almost out of gas.
3. I'm more than kind of
   angry.
4. Relax. We have plenty
   of time.
5. There's lots of room
   left.

Exercise 8

run around
so fond of
What about/or
out of breath/half a
right along
point of
sense of/of us/might even
got an hour/running out of
time
have a lot of excuses
If I run/rest of the
It's a/And you

Exercise 10

1. That idea would upset
   our plans.
2. I should have tried
   harder.
3. You would accomplish
   a lot.
4. We should have eaten
   less.
5. She may have answered
   his letter.
6. That might undo
   everything we did.
7. Would it have been a
   surprise?
8. Shouldn't I be here?

Exercise 11

1. may have been
2. must have done
3. could have had
4. must have been
5. had to have felt
6. would have come
7. could he have thought
8. Would he have gone

Exercise 12

1. could have been
2. could have done
3. out of/matter of fact
4. out of the
5. would have worked out
6. had had/wouldn't have
   been
7. of this/out of/out of
   money
8. could have been of/
   more could anyone
   have done
9. should have started

10. out of/should have
    known

Exercise 13

1. He might have been
   broke.
2. My order should have
   been ready by now.
3. Where could it have
   disappeared to?
4. You might have missed
   it.
5. You should have seen
   what I saw!

Exercise 14

must have bought/ran out of/
must have been leaking/
could have had
wouldn't have/kind of
worth of repairs/should have
written/letter of
be of use
world of experience/would
have found
get rid of it

Exercise 15

1. They must have
   misunderstood our
   directions. (c)
2. What's the point of
   that? (a)
3. It'll take a couple of
   hours. (a)
4. I'm a little out of shape.
   (c)
5. I'm not in favor of it. (b)
6. You had to have been
   bored. (b)
7. Our run left us out of
   breath. (c)
8. He must have been in
   bed with a cold. (a)
9. First of all, it's too
   dangerous. (b)
10. It's a matter of opinion.
    (a)

Chapter 6

Exercise 2

1. brighten
2. lightened

3. something important/
   sitting/reading
4. hidden
5. gotten/starting
6. fountain
7. rotten
8. letting

Exercise 3

1. A: Is it fattening?
   B: Very.
2. A: Why the sudden
      move?
   B: I needed a change.
3. A: There's a meeting
      scheduled at 11:00.
   B: I've something else
      planned.
4. A: They're letting them
      out early.
   B: Lucky for them!
5. A: What's happening?
   B: We're just waiting
      for our order.

Exercise 5

1. We can't afford it.
2. How can he say that?
3. Can you leave
   questions for later?
4. Can't you repeat that?
5. How come she can't
   come?
6. It can happen
   anywhere.
7. I can't finish it so soon.
8. Can't you fix it for me?
9. I can try doing it again.
10. What can have
    happened?

Exercise 6

1. can
2. Can't
3. can
4. Can
5. Can't
6. can't

Exercise 7

1. can
2. can't
3. Can't
4. Can
5. can't
6. Can

Exercise 8

1. He can't have
2. can't seem
3. Can't this be done
4. can have
5. can see/can't believe
6. can go
7. what I can do
8. can I/can clear
9. can't happen/can never
   be
10. can't seem

Exercise 9

1. Where can I get one?
2. I can't even remember
   it.
3. Can we come at
   another time?
4. This can't be it.
5. There's nothing anyone
   can do.
6. Can't they ever agree?

Exercise 10

1. What can't she do?
2. I can't begin to thank
   you.
3. He can't seem to do
   anything wrong.
4. You can say that again!
5. I can't imagine
   anything worse.

Exercise 12

1. but you
2. would you/Could you
3. And you
4. Aren't you
5. When's your
6. Hadn't you
7. Wouldn't you
8. that you're/won't you
9. What did you/what you
10. What are you

Exercise 13

1. costs too
2. test's on
3. lasts
4. ten lengths
5. Five eighths
6. tests you/strongest
   subject
7. fruit tastes/last summer
8. risks

Exercise 14

1. You can't be serious
   about it.
2. It's not what you think.
3. I can carry it for you if
   you like.
4. How did you do?
5. How can they be so
   careless?

Exercise 15

1. A: Did you see the
      Brown's new house?
   B: Yeah. It's something
      else!
2. A: Who are the guests?
   B: Some rather
      important people.
3. A: Are the eggs ready?
   B: They're getting
      there.
4. A: Do you plan on
      waiting?
   B: So long as the line's
      not long.
5. A: Would you like
      something to drink?
   B: Not if it's sweetened
      artificially.

Exercise 16

gotten caught up on
putting them off/end up
owing
waiting to/certainly/wanted
to
a beating/last few months/
starting to
invests at
kidding
all on her own
What do you know/getting to
know

Exercise 17

1. You can't be happy with
   that. (c)
2. Professor Smith can't
   seem to make the class
   interesting. (b)
3. I never take on more
   than I can handle. (a)
4. I can't say enough
   about it. (b)
5. You can't ask for a
   better roomate. (c)

6. How can she be upset?
(b)
7. He can do some work
around here, you know.
(c)
8. You can't insist on
everything your way. (a)
9. What can he say to
that? (c)
10. Can this be the last
one? (a)

Exercise 18

1. *W:* You sure brightened
up when you saw
your test scores.
M: I was worried. I was
in danger of failing
the class.
What are the two
people discussing? (d)
2. *M:* This lasts for
months.
W: Is that a guarantee?
What does the man
mean? (c)
3. *W:* How about getting
together for drinks?
M: Some other time.
What are the two
people going to do? (b)
4. *W:* Let's move the
desks in a circle.
M: What's wrong with
the way they are?
What does the man
mean? (b)
5. *W:* Despite her grades,
Jenny got into
medical school.
M: Wouldn't you know
it!
What does the
conversation imply? (c)
6. *M:* Have you got
something for a
headache?
W: Would one aspirin
do?
What does the man
ask? (a)
7. *M:* Are the new owners
going to make a lot
of changes?

W: They've taken a
wait'n see attitude.
What does the woman
mean? (c)
8. *W:* Would you just
forget it?
M: It's too important.
What does the man
want to do? (b)
9. *M:* When did you get
your coat?
W: Yesterday. And I got
it half off!
What does the woman
mean? (c)
10. *M:* Have you gotten that
proposal in?
W: That's the least of
my worries.
What does the woman
mean? (d)

Chapter 7

Exercise 4

1. I had been
2. not going to
3. At this
4. would guess
5. Has it started
6. about some/on the

Exercise 5

1. just now
2. would be
3. did that
4. made me
5. man-made
6. must be at the

Exercise 6

1. want for/not much
2. get four/on the
3. put these/back seat
would be
4. got the/it comes
5. at this/not right at the
6. that movie/it got better
7. at that/last thing
8. going to/afternoon off/
wish I could join
9. It was stupid of/to have
said that/not that
important

10. think of him/afraid he
would be/last person

Exercise 7

1. I really must be going.
2. *There's a whole
'nother one on the
lower shelf.
3. I doubt that there's time.
4. Let's play it by ear.
5. I thought I ordered it
but I might not have.

Exercise 8

1. That was what she
wanted.
2. It can't have been like
that.
3. Let's start with an easy
one.
4. This could mean a raise.
5. I've never had that
happen before.
6. It would make things
much easier.

Exercise 9

1. He stayed late last
night.
2. I wish I had more time.
3. I wished I had more
time.
4. She's lived for years in
that area.
5. We tried arriving early.
6. It seemed a little out of
character for her.
7. If you need to reach
me, just call.
8. I needed them to help.
9. That shocked all of us.
10. It can't have happened
like that.

Exercise 10

1. He's to arrive there
early.
2. Plant it over there.
3. She works night and
day.
4. She cooked dinner just
once.

*informal English

5. He considers it a problem.
6. He considered it a problem.
7. The school was founded in 1918.
8. He waited long enough.
9. Let's play it safe.
10. He studied the entire time.

Exercise 11

1. helped share/That surprised me
2. skipped classes/on the/ That fits
3. wanted some/realized that
4. that remark/asked what/ wanted
5. advanced math next quarter/complicated subjects
6. worked night/touched by
7. enjoy their/visit often
8. seemed unconcerned/it turned/it mattered more
9. called three/responded to
10. pleased with/thrilled with

Exercise 12

1. A: I need this gift-wrapped.
   B: There's an extra charge for that.
2. A: What's with Jim?
   B: It's not what you think.
3. A: It sure is hot in here.
   B: What happened to our air-conditioned room?
4. A: He got a ticket.
   B: It serves him right.
5. A: That was a wasted meeting.
   B: I'd say so.

Exercise 13

in the

that brand there
That's a lot for
want one
but I hadn't planned on/that much
going on sale next week/ could give
What kind of a
That settles it

Exercise 14

What was/Did something
Not that/just happened to/
not the first time/happened this
That doesn't sound like
just wish/on me

Exercise 16

1. M: You need to relax.
   W: I can't seem to find the time.
   What does the man mean? (c)
2. M: Finished looking over the applications?
   W: All but one.
   What does the woman mean? (a)
3. W: Tell me about the movie.
   M: It wasn't worth seeing.
   What does the man mean? (a)
4. W: I'd give anything for a piece of chocolate.
   M: I thought you were on one of your diets.
   What does the woman mean? (d)
5. W: What are you doing up at this time of the night?
   M: I just can't seem to fall asleep.
   What does the woman ask? (d)
6. W: What a great cut!
   M: Thanks, I had someone different do it this time.
   What are the two people discussing? (b)

7. W: That's the worst looking painting I've ever seen.
   M: C'mon. It's not that bad.
   What are the two people doing? (a)
8. M: Shall we get to the airport early?
   W: Yeah. We'd better play it safe.
   What will the two people do? (b)
9. M: How did the test go?
   W: For the most part easy.
   What does the woman mean? (c)
10. M: I have to be well by the time school starts.
    W: You should be OK by then.
    What are the two people discussing? (d)

Chapter 8

Exercise 1

1. That's/it
2. as
3. If I
4. a/and
5. that/to the
6. Were it to
7. in/in the
8. As I
9. one of the
10. to that
11. on a
12. it off and on

Exercise 2

1. What was that all about?
2. I believe it can be picked up in an hour.
3. Of course that remains to be seen.
4. You should know that's much too much.
5. I thought it would never stop raining.

6. Who would ever say that?
7. I think you're overdoing it today.
8. How does it look on me?
9. Really, that's not the issue.
10. His doing that was unexpected.

Exercise 3

1. You know it happens now and then.
2. Sorry, but I couldn't help but overhear.
3. Really it comes as no surprise.
4. It took half as long as we expected.
5. By now I should be right.
6. Unfortunately it was bound to happen.
7. Wish I didn't feel so overworked.
8. As usual, it didn't occur to them. `

Exercise 4

1. It comes
2. I/that/it
3. that/It
4. That
5. it/it/in the
6. do I/these/For the/out in the

Exercise 5

1. Why the wait?
2. Now that's a good-looking car.
3. Is a day and a half enough time?
4. That's the one I was talking about.
5. It's an unusual idea.
6. Can you give me a hint?
7. Watch out, the motor's on.
8. A careless answer could cost him his job.
9. What do you say we take a break?

10. Thanks to the weather, we can go.

Exercise 6

1. It's the only kind he eats.
2. What if I can't keep up with you?
3. It's as if they didn't see me.
4. The party's on for tonight.
5. It's made out of wood.
6. Let's see if we have time.
7. That's not a decision that's up to me.
8. How they can be so rude is beyond me.

Exercise 7

1. about that/a
2. for the/that I know of/the
3. in that/take care of it
4. That was the/of it
5. to keep her from/of the
6. Even if/At least
7. than to/on his
8. give him a/doubt it/seen him in
9. we see you at the/had had other
10. I leave an hour/As long as it's OK

Exercise 8

1. A: I'm exhausted from all of this.
   B: You and me both.
2. A: Just one more to go.
   B: We'll be finished in no time.
3. A: How about staying one more day?
   B: If anything, I would like to stay a week longer.
4. A: Want to go out for a bite to eat?
   B: Let's stay home for a change.
5. A: Who wants seconds?
   B: Me. But just half of what you gave me last time.

6. A: You're hard to get a hold of.
   B: I've been in and out.

Exercise 9

1. Kim remembered talking with her advisor. (a)
2. Kathy forgot to go shopping. (b)
3. Dave stopped in the hall to smoke. (a)
4. Jane remembers skiing last week. (a)
5. Bob forgot having made an appointment with his client. (b)

Exercise 10

1. Pat remembered to see the doctor before he left on his trip. (b)
2. Karen forgot to pick up the groceries. (a)
3. Joe stopped exercising when his back began hurting. (a)
4. At midnight, George stopped to study. (a)
5. Bill remembered to order the pizza for the party. (b)

Exercise 11

1. It's not our fault.
2. We've done our part.
3. Here are the lists you wanted.
4. It's now or never.
5. An hour or two is enough.
6. What are the chances?
7. You'd better decide or else.
8. How are you justifying that?
9. Two are better than one.
10. It's our least expensive one.

Exercise 12

1. with this/the one over there

2. on/it all the
3. that/that
4. these/the ones/those are not the ones
5. once in a while/You've got to
6. the quarter's over/to go
7. going to work on the/to the/time to time
8. what we/to do/guess is/ at least another/and a half

Exercise 13

1. A: I thought you would be at the party.
   B: At the last minute I changed my mind.
2. A: How did you do on the exam?
   B: It wasn't all that difficult.
3. A: Which of these is better?
   B: I would say the one on the right.
4. A: Isn't there a decision yet?
   B: They keep going back and forth.
5. A: Didn't you remember meeting her?
   B: Not in the least.

Exercise 14

to the
it/Today's a
it's open/one of their/for an/
get out of
a little/pulled a
Is it something/get checked out
But I/any insurance
just started
And it
it

Exercise 15

1. W: We need your decision.
   M: Give me a week or two.
   What does the man mean? (c)

2. M: When will I hear about the job?
   W: The manager will let you know.
   What does the woman mean? (c)
3. W: Why are you keeping quiet about it?
   M: So as not to cause any trouble.
   What does the man mean? (a)
4. W: I have yet to see your new baby.
   M: She seems to grow an inch a day.
   What does the woman mean? (b)
5. M: Should I be late, begin without me.
   W: Sounds good.
   What does the man mean? (d)
6. M: I need a little more time.
   W: Would another week do?
   What does the woman mean? (a)
7. M: I forgot to get Suzanne's address.
   W: I just so happen to have it with me.
   What does the man mean? (d)
8. W: I wish they would turn down the music.
   M: It's enough to drive me crazy.
   What does the man mean? (c)
9. M: Does that include your airfare?
   W: At a cost of $700, it should include the flight.
   What does the woman mean? (b)
10. W: All set?
   M: Just another minute or two.
   What does the man mean? (d)

Chapter 9

Exercise 2

1. He wasn't there on time.
2. You should do more for them.
3. Couldn't he do that himself?
4. We weren't planning on coming.
5. It isn't all that bad.
6. They want to know what time to come.
7. Isn't it worth it?
8. She would know more than anyone.
9. You won't believe what he said.
10. Couldn't that be a problem?

Exercise 3

1. won't
2. want to
3. wouldn't
4. Doesn't
5. weren't
6. does/doesn't
7. shouldn't
8. Is
9. Won't
10. aren't

Exercise 4

1. It doesn't seem to make a difference.
2. That isn't what upsets me so much.
3. To be so late isn't like her.
4. This isn't exactly what I had in mind.
5. Well, doesn't she work indoors?
6. What isn't clear about this?

Exercise 5

1. He did say he'd try to come.
2. It didn't make sense for a while.
3. We did know it would cause a problem.

4. He doesn't understand how to go about it.
5. She doesn't try to be helpful.
6. He does pretend to have all the answers.
7. You didn't recognize it?
8. He doesn't doubt it happened.

Exercise 6

1. You weren't here, were you? (no)
2. They aren't ready, right? (no)
3. You did want to see them, didn't you? (yes)
4. You didn't study, right? (no)
5. He isn't coming. huh? (no)
6. He does have time, right? (yes)
7. You won't be here, hmm? (no)
8. This isn't right, is it? (no)
9. That won't do, huh? (no)
10. He shouldn't go, should he? (no)
11. She hasn't heard, huh? (no)
12. He does speak English, hmm? (yes)

Exercise 7

1. A: Am I late?
   B: To be honest, I wasn't expecting you until noon.
2. A: Aren't those the ones you were looking for?
   B: Almost, but not quite.
3. A: You could get them by Friday, couldn't you?
   B: That shouldn't be a problem.
4. A: I couldn't work like that day in and day out.

B: I couldn't see myself getting used to it either.
5. A: There's time for a break, isn't there?
   B: There had better be!

Exercise 8

1. A: She's amazing, isn't she?
   B: No one has more energy.
2. A: I want to know more.
   B: As do I.
3. A: How was your date?
   B: I wouldn't mind seeing him again.
4. A: I think driving at night would be better.
   B: We won't see as much that way.
5. A: Shouldn't you mention the rent?
   B: It will probably come up sooner or later.

Exercise 10

1. we'll be out of town
2. she'll get back to
3. He'll be with you in a couple of minutes
4. can't stop/I'll keep
5. They'll be leaving
6. I'll say it is
7. I'm coming/I'll probably end up
8. You're calling/I'm afraid
9. We'll start
10. We're not doing

Exercise 11

1. How have (How've)
2. Who have (Who've)
3. What did (What'd)
4. What will (What'll)
5. Where have (Where've)
6. How will (How'll)
7. Why did (Why'd)
8. When will (When'll)

Exercise 12

1. When did he (When'd)

2. Why have we come (Why've)
3. which will (which'll)
4. How did you (How'd)
5. What will we (What'll)
6. How have they (How've)
7. Where have you heard (Where've)
8. What did (What'd)
9. Where did you (Where'd)/What does it (What's)
10. How did you (How'd)/What did you (What'd)

Exercise 13

1. Where's he planning on going? (is)
2. Why's she want to reapply? (does)
3. Who's to know? (is)
4. When's it scheduled for? (is)
5. What's she done so far? (has)
6. How's he supposed to find out? (is)
7. When's the quarter begin? (does)
8. Why's there been such a problem? (has)
9. How's it going to turn out? (is)
10. What's she decided to major in? (has)

Exercise 14

1. How long is it (long's)
2. Why has there been (Why's)
3. When is (When's)/What is wrong (What's)
4. What has happened (What's)/This is (This's)
5. Nobody has come (Nobody's)
6. Why has he not told (Why's)
7. flu is going (flu's)/vacation is (vacation's)
8. what is planned (what's planned)

Exercise 15

1. You didn't say it'd take so long.
2. I didn't promise it'd be ready.
3. I believe it'll be tomorrow.
4. I bet it'd never happen to me!
5. It'll be quite a change.
6. It'll be better than ever.
7. If it'd help, I'll do it.
8. It'd been very unexpected, though.
9. But it'll sound kind of strange.
10. What it'd mean is no work.

Exercise 16

1. How'd you/It'd be
2. I'll try/That'd be
3. How'd the test/Don't ask
4. It'll be/I'm never
5. You'll stay/won't you/ Can't/We're about to/ which'll be
6. room's a/I'd say it

Exercise 17

1. A: Haven't you finished yet?
   B: That'll be the day!
2. A: It'll be expensive to fix, won't it?
   B: Who's to say?
3. A: I guess I'll have to redo it.
   B: Why don't you wait'll later.
4. A: It's not what it looks like.
   B: It'd better not be.
5. A: I don't know how to handle this.
   B: I'm not sure what I'd do either.

Exercise 18

There's a/I'd really/don't remember
it hadn't/wouldn't think we'd have

you couldn't get tickets
That doesn't come
I'll call
I'm a last-minute/I'm sure you've guessed

Exercise 19

1. W: You'll never believe what I saw.
   M: Try me!
   What does the woman mean? (b)
2. M: Think our account's overdrawn?
   W: I wouldn't doubt it.
   What does the woman mean? (a)
3. W: Could I close the door?
   M: I'd rather you didn't.
   What does the man mean? (c)
4. M: If I hadn't seen your car in the parking lot, I would've left.
   W: Didn't I say I'd be here?
   What does the coversation imply? (b)
5. M: Will it hurt?
   W: Just for a minute. But it'll be gone before you know it.
   What does the woman mean? (b)
6. W: Can I borrow your copy?
   M: I don't see why not.
   What does the man mean? (b)
7. M: I didn't exactly catch your name.
   W: I haven't told you.
   Why doesn't the man know her name? (a)
8. W: Only half your order is ready.
   M: That just won't do.
   What does the man mean? (c)
9. W: You'll be ready at 8:00, won't you?
   M: Who knows?

What is the woman implying? (d)
10. M: How's it work?
    W: I wish I knew.
    What are the people most likely referring to? (a)

Chapter 10

Exercise 1

1. He leaves sooner than he planned.
2. That really sounds weird.
3. It'll happen someday.
4. What makes you so sure?
5. Her wishes weren't known at the time.
6. She left town a day ago.
7. He should arrive safe and sound.
8. It looks something like a mosquito.
9. Half the time she looks sleepy.
10. He makes the same mistake time and time again.

Exercise 2

1. Put the dishes away.
2. The machine's on.
3. Her question's too hard.
4. The ice's in the freezer.
5. The test's tomorrow.
6. Seattle's home to Boeing.
7. Bob's sister just came.
8. His wishes are unreasonable.
9. My dad's boss had a breakdown.
10. The bus's long overdue.

Exercise 3

1. He's gotten the mail already.
2. It's been spoken of before.
3. He should take his time.

4. It's better to eat it cold.
5. I have it hidden away somewhere.
6. You sound like a broken record.
7. I just about froze standing here waiting.
8. They stole it from the store.

Exercise 4

1. The company went broke in September.
2. He was chosen from among fifty applicants.
3. They've often spoken of their kids.
4. I don't plan on forgiving him.
5. You're sure you've driven a clutch before?
6. You simply take on too much.
7. I've given that some thought.
8. Her parents give in to whatever she wants.

Exercise 5

1. It's an unspoken rule.
2. Well, that was certainly a wasted morning.
3. What an inviting dinner!
4. That could have been a damaging comment.
5. It's comforting to know that.
6. Why such a puzzled look?
7. Your eye's swollen again.
8. That's classified information.

Exercise 6

1. The pipes are rusting again.
2. The sky is clouding over.
3. You look like you've been sleeping.
4. I wish it weren't so rainy out.

5. I'll be lazing in the sun next week.
6. The rain makes my hair too curly.
7. The roads are too snowy to drive on.
8. It sure is smoky in here.
9. He's risking his job by doing that.
10. She's sunning herself out on the lawn.

Exercise 7

1. These eggs are runny.
2. I feel a little shaky.
3. There's something smelly in here.
4. You could be risking your job.
5. This tastes rusty.

Exercise 8

1. Which is the longer of the two?
2. It's bigger than I had planned on.
3. What's your greatest worry?
4. It's not my strongest subject.
5. Why were you so late returning last night?
6. It's not as fast as I'd expected.
7. No sooner had we arrived than we had to leave.
8. Which word is the closest in meaning?
9. The longer you wait, the more tired you'll get.
10. It's getting harder and harder to see the point.

Exercise 9

1. Nothing is cheaper than this. (a)
2. Prices have never been low there. (b)
3. You won't see a happier baby. (a)

4. I've never met a luckier person. (a)
5. I haven't felt safer. (a)

Exercise 10

1. He's never been friendlier. (a)
2. The need has never been greater. (a)
3. Nothing is simpler than that. (b)
4. At no time will it be easy. (b)
5. It's as hard as I anticipated. (b)

Exercise 11

1. I've never seen it colder.
2. It's as bad as I imagined.
3. It won't get any cheaper.
4. This wasn't my greatest day.
5. The longer you wait, the angrier you'll get.
6. Your guess is as good as mine.

Exercise 12

1. That has ninety calories.
2. He's fourteen years old.
3. I'd like to lose fifteen pounds.
4. They ordered thirty too many.
5. Will seventy dollars do?
6. The war began in 1916.
7. It's some seventy miles away.
8. She can't be eighteen yet!

Exercise 13

1. 1014
2. 30,415
3. 4150
4. 18,160
5. 90,014
6. 80,516
7. 13,770
8. 515,380

9. 703,418
10. 970,990

Exercise 14

1. *A:* How many did you want?
   B: Sixty to seventy would be about right.
2. *A:* What did she get the award for?
   B: She delivers up to fifty papers a day and has never had a complaint.
3. *A:* What date was that?
   B: I believe he died in either 1917 or 16.
4. *A:* If I don't get on Flight 13, I'll miss my connection.
   B: We'll see what we can do.
5. *A:* It expires in eighteen days.
   B: I'll get it renewed.
6. *A:* Why can't you invite more than fourteen?
   B: The restaurant set the limit, not me.

Exercise 15

1. Your directions were unclear.
2. That china's replaceable.
3. What an uncommon signature!
4. However uncomfortable, I'll do it.
5. Don't you think they're acting a little unreal?
6. How illogical can you get?
7. My heartbeat's been more regular lately.
8. That wouldn't be the most convenient time.
9. You expect me to accept something incomplete?
10. Will they take unskilled labor?

Exercise 16

1. an unimportant
2. informal
3. are capable
4. indirectly
5. unmanageable

Exercise 17

1. It's not inexpensive.
2. You're a little unqualified for this.
3. I wear an irregular size.
4. They sure treat us unequally.
5. Your file is incomplete.

Exercise 18

1. with the/any easier
2. to be used/the slightest idea
3. picked a harder/need the
4. signed up/That being
5. sure is getting colder/ winter'll be
6. straightened out/ couldn't agree
7. splitting/aspirin's
8. sleepy

Exercise 19

1. *A:* Can you do it so it's straighter?
   B: I've done it as good* as I can.
2. *A:* Do you need it smaller than that?
   B: Yeah. It's way too big.
3. *A:* I believe the university was founded in 1850.
   B: Huh? You're way off.
4. *A:* How informal can you get?
   B: I thought jackets and ties were a must.
5. *A:* Bill's wife deserves better.
   B: C'mon. You're being unfair.

* informal English

Exercise 20

What do you say
Couldn't we/it's too rainy/
book's/waiting till
We're not going to
That's/opens up
It has in/can't wait to/out of/
couldn't be nicer/for
fourteen days
for a
I'm keeping/fingers crossed

Exercise 21

1. *W:* Do you have this in a larger size?
   M: Size fourteen is as large as they come.
   What does the man mean? (c)
2. *M:* You look exhausted.
   W: I've never felt better.
   What does the woman mean? (d)
3. *W:* You seem to have a busy schedule.
   M: I'm only working part-time.
   What does the man imply? (a)
4. *M:* Does something seem unusual to you?
   W: It's quieter than normal.
   What does the woman mean? (c)
5. *W:* I've never taken an exam as long as that.
   M: Neither have I.
   What does the woman mean? (b)
6. *M:* When do you need this?
   W: Thursday at the latest.
   When does the woman need it? (b)
7. *W:* I've never felt sicker.
   M: You should have eaten less.
   What does the man mean? (d)

8. *W:* That meeting took a
    lot longer than I
    expected.
    M: I've had worse days.
    What does the man
    mean? (a)
9. *W:* Do you have to be
    so impolite?
    M: We're just
    whispering.
    What does the woman
    mean? (b)
10. *M:* You couldn't have
    chosen a harder
    teacher.
    W: How so?
    What does the man
    mean? (c)

Chapter 11

Exercise 1

1. Question
2. Statement
3. Statement
4. Question
5. Question
6. Question
7. Statement
8. Question

Exercise 2

1. It's not our problem?
2. Two hours won't do.
3. He's way above
   average?
4. She's left for the day.
5. On second thought,
   let's say about 8:00?
6. Late again.
7. It's over our heads.
8. You've never had that
   happen before?

Exercise 3

1. That's right, isn't it?
   (uncertain)
2. He's finally finished,
   hasn't he? (uncertain)
3. It's pretty hard, isn't it?
   (certain)
4. She's out of town,
   isn't she? (certain)

5. A good number of
   people are expected,
   aren't they? (uncertain)
6. A couple of days'll help,
   won't it? (certain)

Exercise 4

1. Are you lecturing, Sue?
2. Did it sting Jack?
3. Who's leading, Kim?
4. It's fun to visit Jim.
5. Why did you watch,
   Dan?
6. How did you hear,
   Nancy?

Exercise 5

1. Why are you washing,
   Tom? (b)
2. How much did you give
   Linda? (a)
3. It's easy to hate, Fred.
   (a)
4. When are you leaving
   Sue? (a)
5. It's hard to tell, Jake.
   (a)

Exercise 6

1. It's difficult to like,
   Sam. (a)
2. It's interesting to
   watch, Scott. (b)
3. They are studying Bob.
   (b)
4. Will you visit Billy? (a)
5. It's easy to be fond of
   Sara. (b)

Exercise 7

1. Why did you bet, Mary?
2. Where did you fly
   Mike?
3. It's sad to see, Kevin.
4. What did you make
   Jean?
5. It's not easy to take
   Joe.

Exercise 8

1. a. He's in the
       LIBRARY?
    b. HE'S in the library?

2. a. I'M opposed to that
       idea.
    b. I'm opposed to THAT
       IDEA.
3. a. YOU should see what
       he did.
    b. You should see what
       HE did.
    c. You should SEE
       what he did.
4. a. THAT can be
       finished in a day.
    b. That can be
       FINISHED in a day.
    c. That can be finished
       in a DAY.
5. a. We asked WHEN he
       could come.
    b. WE asked when he
       could come.
    c. We ASKED when he
       could come.
    d. We asked when he
       could COME.
6. a. He said it's on your
       RIGHT.
    b. He said it's on YOUR
       right.
    c. HE said it's on your
       right.
    d. He SAID it's on your
       right.

Exercise 10

1. Did she act strange? (b)
2. How ugly? (b)
3. Did we ever have fun!
   (b)
4. Is this a hard test! (a)
5. Will it be boring? (b)
6. Does it look old! (a)
7. Is that a good picture?
   (a)
8. Did I eat a lot! (b)

Exercise 12

1. That settles it? (b)
2. Haven't you done
   enough? (sarcastic) (b)
3. You were **where** last
   night? (b)
4. Didn't he worry, Karen?
   (a)
5. This is fun, is it? (a)

6. It sounds really cheap, doesn't it? (uncertain) (c)
7. **I'll** wait to see what they have to say? (b)
8. Are you cooking, honey? (c)
9. What's with you? (sarcastic) (a)
10. How can John be so careless? (b)
11. You call that good work? (sarcastic) (a)
12. Can't you do anything right? (sarcastic) (b)

Exercise 13

1. *M:* Won't this lecture **ever** be over?
   W: I think it lasts another hour.
   What does the man suggest about the talk? (d)
2. *W:* Going to pass the driver's test, are you?
   M: I'd better!
   What does the woman imply? (d)
3. *W:* I got **six** weeks off!
   M: A number of people would love to be in your shoes.
   What can be concluded about the woman? (a)
4. *W:* We're supposed to be there at 6:00?
   M: As far as I know.
   What does the woman mean? (a)
5. *M:* I talk too much, do I?
   W: That's what he said.
   What does the man mean? (d)
6. *M:* That the right part for this model?
   W: What do the directions say?
   What does the woman imply? (c)
7. *M:* This is my sister, Jean.

W: I can't get over how much alike you look.
What is the man's relation to Jean? (a)
8. *W:* How boring this is!
   M: You said it!
   What does the woman mean? (a)
9. *M:* How does your company like the new high rise?
   W: No telling what they think.
   What are the two people discussing? (b)
10. *W:* I don't think you want that one.
    M: What do you know? (sarcastic)
    What does the man imply? (c)

Chapter 12

Part I: Sentence Paraphrase

1. How did he do in the interview? (a)
2. When's the assignment due? (c)
3. Are they going to pay our way? (a)
4. May I be of assistance? (b)
5. When are you leaving? (d)
6. Mind if I write a check? (b)
7. I have to run down to the store. (c)
8. Should anyone else call, I'll be downstairs. (d)
9. It's some 50 miles from town. (a)
10. Was anyone else around? (b)
11. What's he like? (c)
12. That's what I had in mind. (d)
13. The price has never been lower. (a)
14. There's no end in sight to the trouble. (a)

15. I had to think twice about it. (d)
16. Why are we always the ones to get asked? (b)
17. His work was completed at the age of 66. (c)
18. For the moment, it's final. (b)
19. Jan corrected the papers and handed them back. (c)
20. The snow is sticking. (a)
21. Let's order out tonight. (c)
22. It's too early to tell. (a)
23. You can say that again! (a)
24. No way would he do that. (b)
25. What if I never find it? (d)
26. Everyone except Tom had an idea. (b)
27. Care for an after-dinner drink? (c)
28. What's she up to? (a)
29. Do you happen to have some change? (c)
30. There's to be a party day after next. (a)

Part II: Short Conversations

1. *W:* Are you done with the project yet?
   M: I have a ways to go.
   What does the man mean? (a)
2. *W:* We'll be on our way.
   M: I wish it weren't so late.
   What does the woman mean? (b)
3. *W:* I can't wait for the end of the quarter.
   M: You and me both!
   What do the two people imply? (a)
4. *W:* How's business been?
   M: Sales have never been better.
   What does the man mean? (b)

5. W: Joe's not here yet.
    M: You know Joe. It's not unusual for him to be a little late.
    What does the man say about Joe. (d)
6. W: I can't tell you how upset I am.
    M: It'll all work out.
    What does the woman mean? (c)
7. W: Thanks for helping me clean up.
    M: It's the least I can do.
    What can you conclude about the man? (b)
8. M: I'm too tired to study.
    W: Why don't you lie down for a while?
    What does the man mean (a)
9. W: More than half the class failed.
    M: That's not usual, is it?
    What does the woman mean? (c)
10. W: Sorry I'm late. I got stuck in a traffic jam.
    M: I was beginning to wonder what happened.
    What does the man imply? (d)
11. W: Can I use the copy machine?
    M: Be my guest.
    What are the two people referring to? (c)
12. W: Is it a three- or four-story building?
    M: I really couldn't say.
    What does the woman want to know? (d)
13. M: Want to go visit Bob in the hospital tomorrow?
    W: Let's play it by ear.
    What are the two people discussing? (d)

14. W: That test was pretty short.
    M: That's easy for you to say.
    What does the man imply? (a)
15. W: Look at Sue's baby.
    M: Before you know it, she'll be a year old.
    What does the man mean? (a)

Part III: Conversation

W: One more screw and I've just about got this clock fixed.
M: Need some help?
W: Yeah, just hold it right there. And can you hand me the other screwdriver?
M: Where did you learn to fix things?
W: From my dad. He was a mechanic.
M: Did he repair cars?
W: No. He worked for the newspaper. He could fix anything. We once took apart a car engine and put it back together again. With so many kids in our family, this was about the only time I had alone with him, so when he asked me to help him, I jumped at the chance. Now I can fix just about anything.
M: That must pay off.
W: Yeah, last week my refrigerator went out. I probably saved over $75 in repairs by not having to call a mechanic.
M: That's good to know. Next time I have trouble, I'll call you.

Questions

1. What is the woman fixing? (a)

2. Where did the woman learn to repair things? (d)
3. Why did the woman help her father? (b)
4. What did the woman say about her refrigerator? (c)
5. What does the woman say about her father? (d)

Chapter 13

Part I: Sentence Paraphrase

1. Everyone must take a test as part of the application. (d)
2. You'll never get a better buy than that one. (a)
3. When am I expected? (d)
4. Whatever the problem, we can manage it. (b)
5. I bought it brand new. (a)
6. It didn't do any good. (b)
7. No wonder you're so worn out. (c)
8. It was 1950, to be exact. (c)
9. I'll do it first thing in the morning. (b)
10. Your call was good timing; I just walked in. (b)
11. Do you want to order some fast food? (a)
12. The school had to have been founded a century ago. (a)
13. Nothing would make me happier than a stay at the beach. (c)
14. This road is worse than the other one. (c)
15. Projects like that waste a lot of time. (b)
16. I know it by heart. (c)
17. You'd better double-check that price. (b)
18. They're asking way too much for it. (b)

19. I'm sick and tired of working so hard. (d)
20. I sold it four months ago. (a)
21. If it's OK, I'd like another. (c)
22. What seems to be the problem? (a)
23. Whether he's chosen for the swim team will depend on his grades. (d)
24. I'm afraid there's nothing available at that time. (b)
25. It's apparent that they want another child. (c)
26. That paper has long done the best job of reporting. (d)
27. I could care less about finishing this project. (a)
28. We've accomplished more than we set out to do this past year. (a)
29. Is it only me or is this room freezing? (c)
30. Give me a call, however late it may be. (b)

Part II: Short Coversations

1. W: We hate to be leaving.
   M: So soon? You just got here.
   What does the woman mean? (c)
2. W: You'll probably have to work overtime this weekend.
   M: I'll do whatever it takes.
   What does the man mean? (a)
3. W: Will this medicine help my cold?
   M: You can't buy anything more effective.
   What does the man mean? (d)

4. M: Are you going to the jazz festival?
   W: I wouldn't miss it. It's supposed to be wonderful.
   What does the woman mean? (b)
5. M: Did you see your ad?
   W: I can't read the small print without my glasses.
   What are the two people referring to? (d)
6. W: How about dinner tomorrow night?
   M: I've a meeting; otherwise I would.
   What does the man mean? (c)
7. M: I'll have this ready in no time.
   W: I appreciate your effort.
   What does the man mean? (b)
8. W: How was your hike?
   M: We got more rain than we expected.
   What does the man mean? (b)
9. M: We'll be able to cook, won't we?
   W: I believe there's a kitchen.
   What does the man ask? (c)
10. W: I can't get over how long it's taking to make this decision.
    M: It's an involved process, isn't it?
    What does the man mean? (a)
11. W: Did you happen to remember my memo?
    M: It completely slipped my mind.
    What are the two people discussing? (c)

12. W: I'm really pleased with your service.
    M: No one cares the way we do.
    What does the man mean? (a)
13. W: John says he's going to quit his job.
    M: That'll be the day!
    What does the man imply? (d)
14. W: Are you busy at the moment?
    M: Make yourself at home.
    What does the man mean? (c)
15. M: Did you already get something for lunch?
    W: Uh-huh. I'm starved.
    What does the woman mean? (b)

Part III: Conversation

W: There's something on your windshield.
M: Looks like I got a parking ticket. I wonder what for. The meter hasn't run out yet. There's still 15 minutes left.
W: It says here that you parked too far from the curb.
M: That can't be. Does it look too far to you?
W: I'm not a good judge of distance. In any case, you've got to pay it.
M: I'm not going to pay. I don't think I've done anything wrong.
W: There's a late fee if you don't. But if you protest in traffic court, they usually reduce it. Especially if you're a struggling student.

M: Parking downtown sure is becoming a headache. I might as well start taking the bus.

W: It may be cheaper in the long run.

Questions

1. What are the two people discussing? (c)
2. Why does the man think a mistake has been made? (c)
3. Why should he pay the fine soon? (a)
4. How can he get the penalty reduced? (b)
5. What might the man do? (c)
6. Where does this conversation take place? (d)

Chapter 14

Part I: Sentence Paraphrase

1. I couldn't help but overhear your conversation. (a)
2. She stopped to check the oil. (a)
3. The bus shouldn't be long now. (b)
4. He's outside at the moment. (c)
5. I'm used to it. (d)
6. Didn't we see you at the park yesterday? (b)
7. You'll have to excuse me for leaving. (c)
8. On second thought, that shirt does go with that outfit. (b)
9. As soon as he was asked the question, his mind went blank. (d)
10. He's by far the youngest to attend. (a)
11. That's the least of her worries. (b)
12. No matter how hard I try, I don't seem to improve. (b)

13. Have you ever met someone so rude? (a)
14. You'll be in and out in an hour. (c)
15. By the time I got to the airport, the plane had left. (c)
16. It'll be held in room 130. (d)
17. Let me know how it works out. (c)
18. I'd better hurry; I'm already running late. (b)
19. I couldn't agree with you more. (d)
20. It goes without saying. (a)
21. You don't know the half of it. (b)
22. Even though she's pregnant, she doesn't plan to take time off from her job. (d)
23. It wasn't so hard after all. (b)
24. I'm tired of waiting all day. (c)
25. Let her write what she wants. (a)
26. I'm afraid the test is sooner than he thinks. (d)
27. Am I mistaken or is it hot in here? (b)
28. She looks older but she's only in her thirties. (b)
29. They're predicting a tie for that race. (a)
30. We don't have many interests in common. (c)

Part II: Short Conversations

1. M: Would you possibly be able to fix this watch?
   W: That shouldn't be too difficult.
   What does the woman mean? (b)

2. M: What if it rains?
   W: Given the weather, I wouldn't be surprised.
   What does the woman imply? (c)

3. M: Why aren't you in class?
   W: I can't get going.
   What can you conclude about the woman? (c)

4. M: Have you tried replacing the bulb?
   W: This one's not burned out yet.
   What is the woman doing? (d)

5. W: What's with you?
   M: It's pressure from work.
   What can you conclude about the man? (b)

6. W: Where can I get this framed?
   M: There's an art shop down the street.
   Where does the woman want to go? (b)

7. W: Whatever happened to Bill?
   M: I haven't seen him in ages.
   What does the man mean? (a)

8. M: You look thoroughly exhausted.
   W: I worked the entire weekend.
   What does the woman mean? (a)

9. M: What on earth is that?
   W: Looks pretty strange, doesn't it?
   What is the couple looking at? (a)

10. W: Do you think two cartons of milk will be enough?
    M: Better get three to be on the safe side.
    What does the man mean? (c)

11. W: I need to check if I turned off the oven.
M: Don't get up. I'll look.
What does the woman mean? (d)

12. M: Who wants seconds?
W: I'm saving room for dessert.
What does the woman mean? (b)

13. W: Bob has offered to help with the casserole.
M: The last thing I need is another person in the kitchen.
What does the man mean? (b)

14. M: After the robbery next door, I had my locks changed.
W: You can never be too safe.
What does the woman mean? (a)

15. W: How can I be of help?
M: Just tell me who's doing what.
What does the man mean? (d)

Part III: Conversation

M: What should I cook for dinner?
W: That reminds me. I've got to run down to the store and pick up a few things before it's closed.
M: Want me to come along?
W: That's OK. I just plan on running in and out. It shouldn't take more than a few minutes.
M: Oh, you'd better get some milk, we're just about out.
W: I never remember—2% or non-fat?
M: 2%. No matter how hard I try, I can't seem to drink the other stuff. It looks like water.
W: But it's a lot better for your health.
M: What do you mean? I'm in great shape. I just had a physical. You should talk. You still smoke!
W: All right, all right. I can see I'd better get out of here before I get another lecture.

1. Where is the woman going? (c)
2. What will she get? (b)
3. What does the man say about 2%? (b)
4. What can be inferred about the two people? (c)
5. Where does this conversation probably take place? (d)